Diary of a New, Fat, Adoptive Dad

by

Daddy Trev

Written by Trevor Davis-Webb

Book I:
The Daddy Trev Diaries

Cover design by Kieran Baker-Webb
Illustrations and colouring-in by Miss Alexis and Master Goblin.
First Published 2020
ISBN 9798610418223
Independently Published

Dedicated to our gorgeous children

Alexis Carrington

and

Little Angel/Goblin Boy

And to my wonderful husband

Daddy Shaun

Without you all, I would be nothing (but I would also look 10 years younger.)

Thank you
To my Mam and Dad who taught me how to be a good parent
To our whole family for their love and support
To Kieran Baker-Webb for designing the cover
To Faye Kirby for being so dedicated and the endless evenings spent preparing us
To Siobhan Thomas (my Sausage Burger Shiv) for the inspiration to finish this work
To Jeanette Muir for the feedback

Introduction

I have never had so many discussions about poo as I have had in my late thirties. Since I became a father, to be exact. I am an expert on it. My pool of expertise also extends to farting. If a conversation in our house doesn't start about poo; it certainly ends as one. I personally don't get the fascination, but I'm guessing anyone who's a parent to a child under the age of six will understand where I am coming from. I find myself starting conversations with other parents about the subject. The strange places you find it in your house. When your blood rushes cold as your newly toilet-trained child informs you that they have just been for a poo all by themselves. I used to be interesting. I used to be able to talk about a wide range of subjects with confidence and often have people belly laughing with my witty remarks. These days, all I seem to talk about is fatherhood, my children and poo. I don't think I would have it any other way.

I used to have nice clothes that weren't covered in handprints and food. I had less wrinkles and more free time on my hands. What did I do with my free time? I can't honestly remember. Our whole world was turned upside down a few years ago, when a little boy and girl came into our lives and filled our world with light, our house with stains (some food, some crayon and some – yes – poo!) and our wallpaper with interesting 'art'. Most importantly they filled our hearts with love.

Identifying as a gay man and growing up in the '80's and '90's, I had resigned myself to the fact that I would never be able to have a family of my own. A family in the conventional sense of getting married and having children to love and raise and spoil as my own. I accepted that I would be a very cool (though festively plump) Uncle Trev or a stylish (though winter-ready insulated) Godparent to one of my friend's children. After all, being a gay man at that time meant that I was not allowed to legally marry. That privilege only came in 2014. Of course, we could procreate if we wished, through surrogacy if we could find a kind lady to spare us a womb (although I was always confused if we both could have been legally regarded as parents.) As gay men we weren't even allowed to adopt children until 2002. But this isn't a book about my struggle as a gay man. It's about my struggle as a parent. Though it's never really been a struggle to be a dad to my gorgeous children. Challenging at times, yes – often – but, ultimately the rewarding reason and purpose I was put on this Earth. My husband (though at the time we weren't actually married) and I were given the world in 2017 when our lives were enriched (and yes, turned upside down) by the arrival of our 4-year-old daughter and 3-year-old son.

Shaun had always wanted children, and after our relationship started, I quickly realised that I was to be an involuntary parent at times – to him! – as he was so excitable and impulsive and so very easily distracted by shiny and sparkly things. I have always been the sensible, 'boring' mirror to his finger-clicking diva persona in my role as the second half of our comedic duo. Shaun doesn't worry about a thing; his philosophy is very 'live for the moment' whereas I can't make any decision without completing a full risk assessment, holding an hour-long meeting and taking several days/weeks/months of deliberation.

Shaun had already filled our home with a colourful menagerie of animals that I had come home from work to meet; dogs, cats, tortoises, chickens, ducks, fish, snakes, hamsters, guinea pigs, and at one time he was even arranging for a baby monkey to be shipped over so he could love and squeeze and play with it - whilst it wore a nappy and slept in between us at night. Thankfully, after getting wind of this endeavour, I soon put a stop to it before he had passed on our credit card details and life savings in his attempt to become Doctor Doolittle.

Our friends have often joked we should build an ark and rename Shaun, 'Noah.' They aren't far off the mark.

In early 2015, our conversations turned to the subject of actual human children. It was something we had both thought about at that point, but after research into adoption, and the realisation that so many children needed a family, meant that for one of the rare times in my life I made a decision fairly quickly. We both wanted to be fathers.

We didn't adopt babies, which is what many couples would (apparently) prefer. In fact, at the start of our adoption journey, we did specify that we would prefer to adopt a baby. Just one child at first and maybe down the line we would adopt again. It turned out that things changed when we saw the profile of a little brother and sister who were 2 and 4 years old at the time.

After applying to adopt, we quickly had a visit from some social workers to speak with us and explain the process. The next 8 months saw us having weekly visits from our social workers to assess us and complete a very large profile on us, which would be handed out to other social workers, for them to see if they thought we might be suitable for any of the children they currently had under their wing. We had to have medicals. We attended a week's training on parenting, child psychology, adoption and potential issues we may face until, finally, we found ourselves sat in front of a panel of around 15 people, who would decide, after interviewing us and reading our profile, if we would make suitable parents. Fortunately, we passed muster and the process of searching for what is called 'a match' began.

Looking through profiles of children was both very strange and difficult. There were so many children, some with very complex needs, whose faces were staring back at us from the pages we were given. There was even a website we could log on to so that we could extend our search. It's an extremely jarring experience. On the one hand it's exciting to be finally looking for your children, but the reality is that you're reading a lot of sad stories and seeing lots of children who have just had the worst start in life and, for whatever reason, you had to say no to because you weren't right for them. And you can't adopt them all, no matter how much you'd like to.

We fell in love with our children through a photograph we had seen of them. In fact, we were so certain that we had found our match, we had to be reassessed again for two children from an older age group (another trip to panel!) Just looking at their photographs and reading a little about their story was enough to almost stop our hearts. Firstly, they looked absolutely *tiny*. And their little smiles in those photographs, provided with their profile, melted us where we sat. I wondered what was going through their young minds when those photographs were being taken – that these photographs would be the ones that lots of people were going to see as they read through their story and decided if they wanted to adopt them.

I was stood in our kitchen washing dishes at our sink when Shaun approached me with their profile. Immediately, I knew that we had to sit down and read this carefully. I don't often show excitement, but let's just say we got straight on the phone to our social worker so she could express an interest on our behalf to their social worker. I can't go into their story as to why they were in foster care; that's their story and therefore not mine to tell. It was enough to make us immediately want to scoop the pair of them up in our arms and cuddle them as tightly as we possibly could. As you will read, the path to where we eventually arrived at, had a few detours and bumps along the way…

Before I proceed, I must to confess to the reader: This book isn't really a conventional book. It's a collection of fond memories throughout a two-year period from adopting our children, to when Daddy Shaun and I finally got married. Initially, I started to jot down funny little things the kids said, because I wanted them to be able to look back through my journal to witness what an amazing journey we all had taken. Looking back over the entries, one thing that strikes me most, is that while the connection we all felt upon meeting each other was instant, we didn't know each other at all. We all fell in love with each other and got to know each other's personalities. It is a completely alien experience being introduced to your children. You spend a few hours with them that first day and come back the next day for a bit longer, then the next and the next until they come home with you to live forever. But this takes two weeks. It's a bewildering experience and very exhausting and not something every parent would experience. You weigh each other up. You surprise each other every day. You fall in love with each other every day and that loves grows so strong. One day you wake up and wonder what ever would you do without them? They become part of you. They fill your life and your soul. That is how every parent should feel about their children. Unfortunately, sometimes, some children don't get that primal, basic nurture and love from their birth parents and they have to be found new families. Some of those children get to have their happy endings – I know that our children have, as Daddy Shaun and I have. But this is all very deep, and perhaps misleading, as this book is not very deep. This book is a chronicle of how we all came to know each other and the journey we took - are still taking – and presented to the reader as a diary of the hilarious conversations and situations our children presented us with.

Our daughter would grow from a very brave, but quite timid little girl, into an absolute force to be reckoned with. She became lovingly known as Alexis Carrington; presiding over her own Dynasty and learning to snap her fingers to get what she wants and assert herself in a classy way; tongue firmly planted in cheek! (She would also surprise us with how kind and mature she was for her age. Acts of selflessness in a 4-year-old must surely be unheard of – but not with our daughter. She is formidable in every way you could imagine.)

Our son would morph from a tiny Little Angel Boy in nappies to a cheeky, little chap called Little Goblin Boy who would throw out some of the best one-liner's I have ever heard (and also turn throwing yourself to the ground and turning a tantrum into an art form – but what a loving little boy our son is – so full of love and joy.)

My husband and I became fathers. Emotions over the years have ranged from pure, unadulterated joy to wanting to dive headfirst into a bubble bath whilst clutching an electric toaster plugged into the mains.

We are all still on this amazing journey today (and I'm still on a diet.) Here is a collection of some of the funniest moments we all experienced as a family in our first two years. As we all got to know each other - the more bizarre and comical our experiences became!

Daddy Trev's Diary

It had taken two years to get to this day. Two whole years since we first applied to become adopters. In those two years we had been assessed, trained, questioned and every facet of our lives had been analysed, discussed and deliberated over. The first year eventually resulted in us being approved to adopt; then another whole year of searching for a potential match for parents and child(ren.) We had seen the profiles of a brother and sister 6 months ago and immediately fell in love with them. They were aged 2 and 4 and their little faces in the grainy black and white photograph of their profile stood out to us like a rainbow in amongst the piles of other profiles of children who were also hoping to be loved by a new family - the way all children should be loved and cared for by their parents. The past 6 months had been an emotional rollercoaster, and we were told initially that the two gorgeous kids we had fallen in love with were already matched to other adopters and that it was full steam ahead for another lucky couple. Deflated, we continued our search until one fateful day we attended, on the suggestion of our amazing social worker, Faye, an Adoption Open Day. We had never been to one and we went feeling hopeful, yet not knowing quite what to expect. We were the first adopters to arrive. There were lots of foster carers, family finders and social workers milling around little booths dedicated to children who had been placed in their care. There were plenty of photographs and stories about these kids who hadn't had the best start in life, and were just waiting for a new family and a fresh start to the rest of their lives. It wasn't a comfortable experience. It was odd. Walking from booth to booth; looking at pictures and chatting about all the very different kids – all with very different stories and backgrounds and needs. Here we were; approved 9 months ago and still childless. We'd expressed interest in a few potential matches at this point; but for one reason or another we weren't deemed right for them or someone didn't think they were right for us. Today then, we were completely overwhelmed. We were told that this open day was very likely the 'end of the line' for most of these children (who weren't present, for obvious reasons) as they were older children when most adopters apparently want babies, or they had very complex needs or they were sibling groups and (apparently) the majority of adopters tend to only want one child. There were 6 booths to visit today. As we went from booth to booth, videos of the kids played on a screen in the background to bring the day to life. The very last booth we came to, we both stopped and looked a little harder at one of the photographs featured. It was a full colour photograph of the same grainy, black and white one that had caught our attention months ago. The brother and sister were needing a new family. We immediately turned to their Social Worker and asked why, when we were told that they were in the process of being 'matched' to another family. Their Social Worker told us that it hadn't gone ahead in the end, and that she remembered us from our own profile which we sent over when we expressed an interest all those months ago. Their Social Worker also said that she had wanted to get in touch with us when the potential first match hadn't gone forward, but she didn't have our contact details and no longer had our profile. Today the heavens aligned. We immediately struck a rapport with their Foster Carer, and he said afterwards that he knew straight away that we were the only Dads for the kids he had been looking after for the past 12 months. We waited for what seemed like hours for their video to take its turn on the screen in the room. As soon as their little faces appeared - brought to life with a short film - we just knew they were our children. By the end of the film the room was silent, except for us – and our Social Worker, Faye - in tears. We wanted to go and pick them up and take them home with us immediately. They were perfect. They were our kids. We turned around to see their social worker and foster carer beaming from ear to ear. This was a magical moment, not for the last time, and their foster carer held out his hand to shake ours and declared with the biggest, beaming smile 'have we got a deal, then?' Well... of course the answer was 'YES! YES! YES!' But as excited as we were, we had to come down to Earth and get back to the reality which was that these things take a hell of a long time, and there was still a long path on this journey to travel. That particular part of the journey would take 3 months – and, it wasn't a smooth ride. From the outside, and to us at the time, this all seemed quite a 'clinical' process; almost like a business transaction. It was a very strange scenario to be in, but the gravity of the situation isn't lost on anyone. The main aim is to find these children a new family so they can be loved and feel safe. There's no time or need to beat around the bush. A job has to be done. For the children.

The following week, our social worker sent over our profile and the ball was rolling. Our kid's team were happy - we were happy - but a few weeks later we were told it was all off the table. We were devastated. Apparently, someone allegedly related to them had come forward and had asked to be assessed to adopt them, albeit a full year since they had been removed from their birth parents. We were advised to start looking again. We just couldn't do it. We decided that we were going to put our search for a family on hold for a while as it was too emotionally exhausting to get to that point again. As strange as it sounds, for two children we hadn't even met, it felt like we were grieving for a loss of some sort. We had seen so many photographs of them, watched videos of them, had read so much about their lives so far – it felt like they were already our children. As it turns out – a month after that, we were informed that it was all back on with us in the seat as a potential match, because the relative that had come forward just wasn't suitable. Weeks and weeks of meetings and paperwork and decisions and sign offs progressed until - finally - one day in June 2017 we found ourselves in a room full of professionals who would eventually decide that we were a perfect match for our two little miracles. This was called Matching Panel. Although an intensely important meeting, we felt far more relaxed this time than we did when we had our first experience of Approval Panel. Lots of genuinely smiling faces were looking back at us that day as they approved our match and gave us the go ahead to meet our children. Of course, we had visits to our house to make sure we had child proofed everything, that our smoke alarms worked, that our chihuahua's had been risk assessed, that the brand of soup we had in our cupboards was Heinz etc. Finally! This was it!

The day we met our kids for the first time.

We had been waiting for this day for a long time. We had made books for our little girl and boy with photographs of their new dads, home and dogs in, and their foster carers had video recorded their reactions on reading the books for the first time to them. It was magic. We played those videos over and over again watching the kids watching us for a whole week before we met them. We sent over a couple of short videos of us, as we gave them a virtual tour of their brand-new bedroom waiting for them, so they could see us and hear us in real life. Again, the foster carers played the videos for them and then videoed their reactions and sent them to us. Immediately we could tell our little girl was nervous. We were essentially taking her away from her home and from the people she had grown to love because they had kept her safe and loved for the past 14 months. So much had already happened in her short little life and this was another time where she would have to start again in a new home; new family, new school, new smells – how daunting must that be? Even so, the foster carers had prepared them both so well and they were very excited to be getting two new Daddies (A dad each is how our little girl put it. Apparently, when she had been told they were getting TWO daddies, she ran upstairs to excitedly wake her little brother up from his nap to squeal 'WE GET A DAD EACH!)

Our little boy was so excited in those videos. His 2-year-old little face lit up when he saw us and there was gasps and squeaks of excitement. He clearly could not wait to meet us and seemed bursting with pure joy and excitement at the prospect of it. As excited as we both were, we just didn't know what to expect on that first day we met them.

We had baked cupcakes and cookies for our arrival. We pulled up in the car at 1pm outside the foster carer's house. Nervous and giddy, we walked up the steps to their house in a bit of a haze. From the steps we could only just make out two little blonde heads bobbing up from the sofa by the window - barely big enough to reach to see us. The front door was already open for us and we walked in....

Our babies were in the living room, which was to the right of the front door, so it meant that they were out of sight to us until we turned and walked in. We walked through the door, both of us holding a tray of baked goods for everyone. There. They. Were! Our lives and future stood so impossibly tiny in front of us. As soon as we walked through the door, our little boy ran towards us screaming 'DADDDDD!!!!!' with both of his arms wide open. My legs turned to jelly, and I crouched down to greet him. All I could think to say was 'WOW' - but it was more of a whisper. He squeezed the life out of me. 'I've missed you,' he said, and the sheer joy in his baby voice really twanged our heartstrings. It didn't matter that we'd never met him before. He had seen the videos we had sent and had the books we made read to him - over and over again - and slept with the teddy we had bought for him. We knew what he meant. As far as he was concerned, we had always been his Dads (he would say months later that we were just busy working; getting his bedroom ready, which is why he had been with his Foster Carers. That's how his little mind had made sense of everything.)

I looked over to our little daughter stood cautiously next to her foster carer; her little face looked so nervous – she was looking to him for his approval. He encouraged her to come over to us. She got a bit upset and left the room for a little cry. It was completely understandable. She had lived here for over a year; it was the first time in her short life that she had felt safe and warm and here we were to take her to her new home – albeit her forever home, but how could a four-year-old possibly be expected to be able to process that? Immediately we felt torn between a little boy so overwhelmingly happy to have a new family - and wanting to pick him up and play with him - to wanting to rush out of the room after our daughter to comfort her and cuddle her and reassure her and get to know her. We had completely different reactions from the both of them.

After a couple of minutes, she came back into the room and cautiously made her way over to us. She offered Shaun a building block and said it was a dinosaur she had made out of blocks. He gently received it with a huge smile, and she plonked herself right on his lap as we sat on the floor, seemingly to claim her Daddy. She started to giggle and play with the three of us. It took her a little longer than her brother, but after a few minutes we were all playing outside on their bikes; laughing and carrying on together rolling around in the grass. I should point out that this is all going on as the foster carers and social workers were sat watching and observing (with huge smiles all round!) I felt like I was on Britain's Got Talent and any minute Amanda Holden was going to press her buzzer! In all honesty we forgot they were there. They all very quickly realised that the four of us had all clicked together like a jigsaw and they left us to our own devices for the next two hours. We only got two hours with them that first day. It was the most exhausting, bewildering, overwhelming day of our lives at that point. Truly amazing. Neither Daddy Shaun or Daddy Trev knew exactly what to expect from this point on, but what a strange, magical (and comical) journey it was going to be. For the next two weeks, we were to visit every day until they would come home to live with us.

This week we have so far had, trips to the park, carpet picnics, soft play, and today was the first time our kids came to our house – correction THEIR new house - for the day. Our (collective) house was littered with toys, books, paints, and the garden was turned into a magical kingdom with bubble machines and a climbing frame and music playing. We had even converted the shed into a bright pink princess castle! Promptly informed by our little girl that it was amazing, but wasn't a real princess house because it didn't have the right kind of door and also didn't have a bridge! Shaun swiftly contacted the local landscapers and applied for planning permission to dig a moat.

They were accompanied by their foster carer and we waited nervously in the living room as they ran up the drive, all smiles. They burst through the door and ran up to us – so excited to see us and their faces were just a picture when they went into the garden. It was like a scene from a CBeebies panto! They were ecstatic. Their foster carer was over the moon for them and didn't stick around to make sure they were OK – he knew they were just fine.

'Dads, come and catch bubbles with us!!!' Excited battle cries from our little girl. Orders have been given. Off we go to catch bubbles.

I have been called many, many things in my life. Some good, some unkind, some way off the mark. I've been called handsome, ugly, fat, skinny, son, friend, mate, gay boy… you name it.

However, I have never been called Dad until now. When your son and daughter call you Dad and Daddy - it's just the most amazing feeling. I just melt.

Our son also calls us both Poopy Head. He's so articulate for a 3-year-old.

We were introduced as Dad and Daddy (Shaun was Daddy, and I was Dad.) However, this seemed a tad confusing for such young little souls, so we decided it was easier and less confusing for them if we got them to call us Daddy Trev and Daddy Shaun. It also seemed odd for our kids to keep asking 'which one are you? Dad or Daddy.' They needed our names!

We are very quickly becoming experts on 3-year-old tantrums. In fact, I'm thinking about having it as my chosen subject for when I apply for Mastermind.

Latest meltdown from our little boy:

'Daaaaadddddddyyy, my ice pop is too collllllllllllddddddddd...'

He then proceeds to blow on it to make it cool enough to eat, with tears rolling down his little cheeks.

Of course, he won't be 'advised' that this isn't the way to warm up an ice pop, because he knows everything, naturally. I just give him a cloth to hold his ice pop with and a truce seems to have been agreed…for now.

It is also time for our very first sleepover tonight. We have all been so excited. We all had our new pyjamas on and sat down to watch the Trolls movie, complete with brand new Princess Poppy and Branch teddies for our angels. Sat with popcorn and sweets and fizzy pop with our curtains closed and blankets over us to create that cosy atmosphere. It's also one of the hottest days of the year and I'm actually gasping for air, but the feeling of being safe, secure, warm, content, happy and a family is the best feeling in the world. We tucked them in tonight singing away songs from the movie we had just watched and reading them bedtime stories. They were in their absolute element. This feels so right. This feels like family. They both slept right through and didn't murmur all night.

Daddy Shaun and I, however, didn't sleep a wink. We kept listening out for them. Parents at last.

I've clearly turned into one of those people who gushes daily about my kids.

Today's little random nugget:

Our son: 'Daddy, I can't lick my feet!!'

Me: 'Erm, I know???'

Him: 'Because I'm not a dog, Dad.'

Well, I certainly can't argue with that one! I can tell that this kid is gonna go far!

After all the training and preparation we did to become parents, there were a few things we weren't told:

1. We need to spend at least 3/4 of our whole day ready to 'watch me, Daddy!' or 'watch this, Dad!'

2. It can take 15 minutes for a 3-year-old to put on shoes (because 'let ME do it!') but 8 seconds to delete 76 photos, 3 apps and change the language setting on my phone from English to ancient Sanskrit.

3. Lasagne nappies are as close to a near death experience as I ever want to get. Oh, my days! What a mess! Must also learn to add less garlic next time.

Do you know what else? We feel like we've won the Lottery.

We're on the final day of the 'Introduction Period' and after sleeping over at our house again last night, we must drop our kids back off with the foster carers this afternoon as they have planned a goodbye tea for them. They will also sleep over at the foster carers tonight for the last time, and tomorrow morning, after a quick meeting, we go and pick them up for the final time and drive home to start our lives together. It feels odd dropping your children off with the foster family. We didn't want to, given that they have practically lived home with us for the past week, but it's important to them all that they have a chance to say goodbye and to have a bookend on this particular chapter. They both had fantastic foster carers, too. Seriously great people.

This afternoon, an 'Adoption Shower' party has been planned for us and all our family and friends have gathered to give us and our children gifts and money. Seems strange to think that we'll all be having separate parties this afternoon and even stranger that all the people we love at our party won't even get to meet the kids for weeks yet. We have to slowly introduce close family over the next month so it's not too overwhelming.

My little girl struts into the room, with an outfit on that we will call a 'choice.' It seems to comprise of a dress with a feather boa, Minnie mouse glasses and every item of plastic jewellery she could find.

She comes over and enquires: 'Dad, have you seen that book?'
Me: 'Which book?' (She's got a full library!)
Her: 'The big one.'
Me: 'What's it about?'

she stares at me blankly

Me: 'What's in it?'
Her: 'ummm, lots of pages.'

Stupid me!

I'm only new at this parenting game, but I have an AMAZING tip for anyone cleaning up after feeding a 3 and 4-year-old spaghetti bolognese. It saves so much time, and can be achieved with maximum results in just 3 easy steps:

Step 1: Remove yourself, your children, your pets and other loved ones from the property (don't forget the tortoise – he's called Fluffy, if anyone is interested to know.)

Step 2: Douse the dining room/kitchen in petroleum.

Step 3: Light match and leg it as fast as your high heels will carry you.

It's so simple and effective and I think it really will just save time on cleaning the mess that was created.

We are so grateful to everyone for everything they gave the kids at the adoption shower. The kids had a great day today spending their money - especially in Toys R Us.

Our little girl got this 'Frozen' ice cream parlour. Which came flat packed. Which we assembled (I say 'we'; I mean ' Daddy Shaun')

Our advanced engineering degrees and knowledge of physics sure came in handy when putting this together! Our special superpowers of being able to decipher - and master! - SEVERAL different languages simultaneously, within minutes - was a big help when it came to the 'instructions.'

Our patient princess helped along the way, while the HOURS of fun putting this up flew by ('Daddy, is it ready yet? Dad....Dad....Dad.....DAAAAADDDD!!! Is it ready yet?')

Eventually it was all assembled and our girl was open for business! And she meant business! It came with a till, card machine and pretend coins! However, she wanted cold hard cash for these pretend frozen treats! And we had so much pretend ice cream, and she had so much cash she could probably retire soon. She also has our chip and pin and doesn't accept American Express.

When asked if she liked the new present we bought her, we were promptly advised 'but I bought it!' Which, to be fair, she did hand the cash to the lady at the tills. She'll be on The Apprentice in a few years

Daddy Shaun's turn for the morning shift. Daddy Trev gets an extra hour in bed.

The morning shift includes; last night's tea being cleaned away from our son's bottom; what a true delight and rare treat (up until now) it is to clean away poo at 6.45am when your eyes are still glued shut with morning sleep.

The morning shift also includes supervision of breakfast; not much eating going on at our table, though.

Daughter age 4: 'I can't want that' (This is a term she will repeat like a mantra whenever some offending food is proffered to her. I 'can't' want that will become her catchphrase! On this occasion, the food presented which seems to cause such an outrage is… Shock! Horror! Gasp! Watermelon!)

Daddy Shaun: 'What you mean is you don't want that. Well if you don't try that; the breakfast fairies might be very sad and won't bring special things to the table anymore. Also, if you don't try that you won't be able to have any of the chocolate shoe.' (The chocolate shoe was made, with love and by hand, the previous evening by Daddy Shaun instead of putting his feet up after a hard day parenting.)

Daughter: 'That shoe is not chocolate - it's a shoe!!'

She shrugs her shoulders and looks at Daddy Shaun as if he should be sent to the corner with a Dunce hat on.

'Chocolate is brown', she asserts. (Granted, it was a white chocolate shoe Daddy Shaun had lovingly spent hours constructing the night before.)

While this conversation is going on, our son, aged 3, is making pretty patterns with Coco Pops across the table - bathing himself in milk (an early multitasker! YES!)

Anyway, today's lesson at breakfast was "feelings."

Daddy Shaun showed them, with facial expressions, what happy is, sad and angry etc. They copied his actions and he then told them when they feel angry or sad to talk to Daddy Trev or Daddy Shaun.

Daddy Shaun explained that sometimes when you're angry or sad, Dads can help you to be happy again.

3 minutes and 18 seconds later, son age 3, starts yanking at the play-room door in anger 'I want it open - I want it open NOW!'

Daddy Shaun: 'No, it's too early. We are going to have breakfast first.'

Our Little Angel Boy then proceeded to scream and shout and run on the spot stamping his tiny feet. Daddy Shaun explained to him that this feeling was "anger" and we all wanted to be happy today. We then saw our opportunity to show off our training we had been given, and really go for it in the parenting skills department by using The Distraction Technique; I quietly told his sister she was such a good girl and we were going to watch cartoons.

He is now glued to Paw Patrol happy and silent. (Little Angel Boy, not Daddy Shaun, for clarification.)

Morning shift almost over. Can't wait for their nap time - so we can have one too!

I've said 'no' so many times this last couple of days (every few seconds or so) that I'm not surprised our 3-year-old son keeps having a meltdown every time I say it because I'm starting to annoy myself by saying it.

Things we've said 'no' to him for:

Looking at and touching his own poo.
Looking at and touching the dog's poo.
Driving us all to the park. In our car.
Drinking the bath water.
Thinking the bathroom floor is the place to spit out the bath water.
Drawing on the patio doors.
Eating the chalk he used to draw on the patio doors with.

He's a good lad though and we love him and his sister to bits!

I just have to take a moment, sometimes, and sit back and watch them both in awe. They are so brave and resilient and have endured and coped with so much change in their short, little lives that it's hard to forget they are only babies. They are our babies. We are still pinching ourselves.

We've been invited for a luxurious complimentary afternoon tea at the castle tomorrow, aka: The local posh wedding venue.

God help them all. We will have a 3-year-old screaming the place down within minutes because the cake stand isn't blue, or because the sandwiches aren't his favourite or cut into the shape of a cat.

He will have food splattered across the luxurious white cloth and paint the seats with whatever food is the most colourful, whilst passing gas from both ends at the table.

But he will love every minute of the experience, whilst our 4-year-old princess sits delicately sipping her tea, carefully not dripping it onto her new frock.

Oh, how time flies in our house! Two amazing, beautiful kids but complete opposites in every way.

If, for any reason, you want to make a 3-year-old boy run upstairs screaming and crying his eyes out then I have just discovered the perfect way:

When he tells you to take your sock off for no apparent reason (just one, in this case the left foot) then just say 'no, why?'

So effective. And you really don't have to do that much.

To escalate to a full-on tantrum, always remember to ask if he wants supper!

August 24 2017 ·

Well, Big Dude Clothing came up as a suggested post on Facebook for me today.

Big Dude.

Big. Dude.

It's a polite term for Fat Mess.

Also, my son was watching Peppa Pig the other day and Daddy Pig came on and he shouted (far too excitedly for my liking) 'Dad, that's you!'

Body shamed by a 3-year-old.

Need to go back to Fat Club and shift some timber. I'll do it right after I finish a family bag of Maltesers.

August 27 2017 ·

We are happy to be fathers to two amazing, kind, polite stunning babies. We completely adore them.

It's crazy what 5 weeks can do, it's transformed us as people, transformed our lives for the better.

Daddy Shaun has gone from being a preened, handsome, smartly dressed lad; obsessed with his appearance; worrying if he didn't have 42 clean ironed t-shirts, 20 pairs of clean trainers, to a slightly dishevelled dad.

Daddy Trev has been in the same tracksuit for two weeks and seems to have forgotten what a comb looks like. I look like I have been thrown down a flight of stairs, backwards, and been left in my own stench for 3 days and when the fire brigade finally break-in I am dehydrated and tearful; deliriously mumbling something about needing six Mars bars.

We now only care that our kids have nice clothes, love, comfort and happiness. But, also, we are too exhausted to care what we even look like anymore.

We're always buying them new things and watching their every move. I literally think I live in their brains - I know what they're thinking - I swear it!

I love the sweaty cuddles after naps; their cries when they are hurt because it makes them cling to me. Then, you feel guilty for thinking that.

We don't care how we look; what we wear; if our trainers are grubby or we don't have the latest fashion. We only care that our kids are happy.

We love life, love our kids and our family.

We are all truly blessed.

August 28 2017 ·

Another dad tip from me.

When you're nearly 20 stone (like me) and you decide to play on the bouncy castle with your kids (who weigh about 3 stone between them), then don't jump on the bouncy castle with such enthusiasm as you will launch them into outer space!

September 3 2017 ·

You've never lived until you've watched 'Pirate Pete does a Poo on the Potty' over and over and over and over and over again! It's a rare Sunday morning treat.

However, there is still no 'movement' on the actual toilet from our little lad. Despite us making a little song to sing, complete with a little dance on the landing, to encourage him to do his business there. He has managed to crouch under the dining room table and fill his Georgie Pig pyjama bottoms, though. Daddy Shaun had fun cleaning that one up. Poor Georgie Pig pyjamas had to go in the bin.

It started after being sat watching him on the toilet trying to coax out a poo from him, like a snake charmer with a basket and a flute. Nothing.

We all went back downstairs and I suddenly realise that our little boy has disappeared from the room, and I can hear 'grunting.'

I do my best Mulder and Scully impersonation and my detective skills track down the grunts to our little boy squatting under the dining room table in his pyjamas. He suddenly catches my eye.

'Leave me alone!!!!!' he whines!

'But what are you….' I don't get to finish my sentence. The stench slaps me right in the face.

He's done it. He's filled his new Georgie Pig pyjamas - which, handily, have elasticated cuffs around the bottom of his legs.

A pair of scissors to cut the PJs off in a vain attempt to minimise mess, and a long showering down later, and my little lad comes up to me and gives me a little smile and dilates his puppy dog, saucer-like brown eyes and I give him a huge cuddle.

Our little girl's first day at Primary School Reception today. It's been emotional, wonderful and all a bit of a blur.

I spent about three-and-a-half hours in Matalan the other week because it was so daunting; the sheer amount of different things you can get for school!

I have spent many more hours shopping online and in other stores and shoe shops. We tried every shoe shop because as new parents we wanted to know what was out there.

Clarks, H&M, Asda, Peacocks, M&S, any way we had a good look around.

Just as we felt like we had nailed everything and that the first day of school was a resounding success, we realised we had sent our little girl to school this morning in a boy's polo under her pinafore and oversized tights. I have no idea how this happened as I spent so much time researching everything, mainly via phone calls to my victims (also known as Experienced Parents.)

On the plus side, I spent another £70 today and I have enough uniform (the correct ones, too) to last the year (not just for our children, but for their whole class!)

I still don't get what socks and tights go with what skirt or pinafore, though.

Our princess came home from her first day of big school full of beans, full of confidence and a different little girl. Even had a different cardigan on – a cheaper version of the one she was sent to school in. She loved every minute. She loves us so much and missed us all, apart from her little brother, obviously.

My Mam used to use a phrase 'shit from arsehole to breakfast time.' I never really knew what it meant...until today.

Our boy has finally started to do a poo on the big boy toilet! Yay!

No fuss! Yay!

Goes without prompting. On his own! Yay!

Attempted to wipe his own bum.... before we got to him. OH! DEAR! LORD!

Little poo fingerprints all over the joint. Toilet seat, sink, taps... it will take us until breakfast time to get it cleaned up.

Now I understand what my Mam meant all those years ago.

Still... big boy toilet. I feel like getting my son to poo on an actual toilet may just be the greatest achievement of my life to date. The constant watching of a nappy-less child wandering freely around the house, the inane little song of 'Poo, poo on the toilet' complete with a dance that has caused a trapped nerve in my fat neck and a prolapsed disc in my spine. It was all worth it! I'm going to add it to my Curriculum Vitae as both a skill and a hobby!

September 13 2017 ·

Just some observations on modern day children's cartoons:

Peppa Pig is a spoilt little bitch.
Norman Price from Fireman Sam is an absolute dickhead.
Horrid Henry isn't just horrid – he's a little arse hole.

Where are the Thundercats and He-Men for this generation?

September 15 2017 ·

In an attempt to raise my boy to be respectful and polite to his elders, a conversation happened today:

Me: 'don't be cheeky to Dad.'

Him: 'OK, Poopy Head.'

Me: 'OK WHAT?'

Him: 'OK, Poopy Dad.'

Whilst this is amusing now, I am having panic attacks for when he reaches his teenage years.

He is going to evolve into an outstanding teenager. I can see it now. He says, when he grows up, he wants to be a fireman in the mornings and a policeman in the afternoons.

Alexis Carrington hears us having this discussion – she has bat-like hearing when it comes to conversations she simply MUST be privy to. She would like to make an official statement regarding her future endeavours in adulthood. She will be an artist during the day and a rock star at night, apparently. Daddy Shaun and I have been promised we can see her concerts for free when she performs. Little Angel Boy may have to re-think his dreams of becoming a member of the Emergency Services, as Alexis requires him to be a backing dancer at her shows.

Our babies. Not so small anymore, as our little boy
started nursery this morning.

The kids have started informing us what they want Santa to bring them for Christmas. It's narrowed down to the first six aisles in Toys R Us and every single advert for kids toys they've ever seen. I hope Santa can carry all this on his Ford Focus sleigh.

I found my Emergency Twix under my pillow this morning. It's going to be a great day.

Dad observation on tantrums (again):

Your 3-year-old will have a proper meltdown if you blink too loudly. Be especially careful not to blink at all, as this will cause the 3-year-old's feet to stamp wildly on the spot and real tears to emerge from their own eyes (which will be selfishly blinking even though YOU'RE not allowed.) Don't even dare to make eye contact with him at this point. It seems to be the source of his power.

Doors/windows/cupboards MUST be opened/closed on command or at will to avoid further instances of the above! I really don't understand why he asked me to open and close our kitchen cupboards at his whim, or even why I did it. But after ten minutes of it, I said it was time to go into the living room, and you would have thought I had asked him to chop his own arm off. The screams that came from his little lungs could well have perforated my ear drum this evening.

September 23 2017 ·

You realise what's important and precious in life when you become a father. I have learned a lot about myself and what I want to teach my kids about the world and life in general. One thing I will teach them is never to enter Primark at 10.30 on a Monday morning in this town as it's full of desperados returning the clothes they've worn over the weekend as they've spent up on the Strongbow Mixed Fruits and now need money for Bingo tomorrow night.

Anyway, deep fatherhood stuff...

I feel ready for the rest of my life.

I feel ready to go back to work.

Also, because Statutory Adoption Pay is peanuts and I'm poor; I'm also ready to be involved in an accident that wasn't my fault, and could be due compensation for.

September 26 2017 ·

Can anyone help out with a risk assessment for a fat man trying to wash his feet in the shower? He used to take baths but, due to constraints on his time with 2 new kids, he is forced to try and balance his fat self; whilst rinsing his trotters with soap now. Asking for a friend.

September 29 2017 ·

Playing Fight List with **Daddy Shaun** and the category is 'Famous Painters.' Daddy Shaun asks 'how do you spell Roald Dahl?'

'Tis a blessing he's pretty.

October 12 2017 ·

We're going through lists of the kids from school with our little girl to see who she wants to invite to her birthday party. Apparently, she plays with and is best friends with, 60 out of the 61 kids. Seems odd considering she can't even tell us who she has dinner with most days.

Anyway... we're not inviting 60 kids. It's just not happening. So, any ideas how we select kids for the most popular girl in school - any school, ever?

She's VERY excited, by the way. She's swanning around the room like a 4-year-old Alexis Carrington overseeing a board meeting at her empire. Definitely Daddy Shaun's daughter.

Maybe we should do it Hunger Games style? Just place the invitations in the middle of the playground and let natural selection do the rest!?

October 13 2017 ·

'Dad, where's that piece of paper thing I had 6 weeks ago?? You had it. I neeeeed itttt. Nowwwwww.' Alexis Carrington is certainly coming into her own now that she has two personal assistants at her beckon call. Three, if you count her little brother, which I'm sure she does. I feel like the assistant girl in The Devil Wears Prada had it easy.

October 13 2017 ·

Daddy Shaun's been organising party bags for Alexis Carrington's 5th birthday. (She has nodded in approval and dismissed us for the day.)

It's not like him to go overboard, but let's just say that the lucky kids attending this party will be leaving with a Rolex, some diamond earrings, the keys to a Mini

Cooper and a two-week holiday to Montserrat in their party bags.

He's toying with the idea of giving them a three-bedroom Barratt starter home, but what with me getting Statutory Adoption Pay things are a bit tight.

Help!

When your kids get a lolly and hand it to you for a minute and say 'look after this for me, Dad.' Do you eat it? To stop it from melting!?
Asking for a fat friend.

Alexis Carrington has been on form today. She's floated around in a tiara and princess gown all day. She's been chauffeured to a private party, and picked back up again. After a few peeled grapes for supper, she'll be off to bed.

She usually says 'goodnight, Dad. Love you.' But tonight, I'm half expecting her to 'shoo' us both away whilst flicking both her hands towards us to motion us out of the door and say 'that's all...'

In other news, our precious little boy has been promoted to top of the class in 'stroppy 3-year-old tantrums.' Bless him. Apparently, it is completely acceptable to cover the dog in Sudocrem and you should <u>not</u> be challenged about this decision whilst you are in the process of creating your art.

October 15 2017 ·

Today marks the second time in 3 months that I've been out of a tracksuit and ran a comb through my hair. I haven't had a haircut in 3 months, so I resemble a homeless (and fat) Victoria Wood with shades of Anne Widdecombe and undertones of Cornetto.

October 17 2017 ·

We've just found out Alexis Carrington's Harvest Festival is in the morning and she's singing in it. I put a tin of out-of-date Aldi tomato soup in her school bag and Daddy Shaun has quickly removed that and stripped our cupboards BARE and is also thinking about turning up with a deluxe hamper from M&S now that we are attending. God forbid any of the other parents out-do him.

He's demanding to know the locations of my Emergency Twix, Emergency Topic and Emergency Peanut Butter Chunky Kit Kat, but I've relinquished my Emergency Biscuit Boost and I can do no more!

Our precious boy has cut his own hair at nursery today. Huge chunk! He's definitely got an eye for this and may end up as the next Vidal Sassoon! His speciality haircut at the moment seems to be 'bicycle helmet meets '80's punk Grace Jones' judging by how he's done his own.

His 'fringe' now seems to start at the back of his head. A definite talent!

Oh. Dear.

In other news, Alexis Carrington ate all of her tea tonight and wants a press release announcing this to all the major tabloids.

Today is being classed as a success!

The beef has been in the slow cooker since last night. It's going to make a lovely dinner tonight. I pray, pray, pray to JESUS that Alexis Carrington is in the mood for beef and it meets her requirements. She's quite particular. We're very nervous.

This is a girl who has cheese and crackers as her dessert at school every day. Our daughter has a cheeseboard every day. A cheeseboard. She's 4.

Dinner update:

The beef seemed to go down well, as we named it 'Special Chicken' to avoid complete melt downs. A couple of sprouts were consumed and all seemed to be to Alexis Carrington's satisfaction. We'll await her full review in the Primary School Reception newsletter.

Our little angel boy seemed to enjoy it, too. So much so that he seemed to be practising his letters in the gravy. All over the table! And he clearly wanted to show us how he painted at nursery today. Except the paint was gravy and his canvas was his clothes, hair and face. And floor. And walls…

Another triumphant day, I'd say. We just need to repaint and re-wallpaper the dining room now and then we can rest for the night.

October 19 2017 ·

The kids had chocolate cake and custard for supper 10 minutes ago. Our boy had TWO portions. I've just sat down with my chocolate cake now with a bit of custard on the top and our boy runs over and sits on my knee, licking his lips, and blowing on it for me as it's hot. He's three so when he blows something to cool it down, it's not just air that comes out of his mouth.

He says (pointing to my custard): 'Dad, what's that on top of your cake?'

I reply: 'your spit, now.'

His reply: 'let me try now, Dad. You have to share.'

I can't believe he's throwing that rule back in my face when it suits him!

Alexis Carrington was naughty this morning so her afternoon engagements for tomorrow have been cancelled as punishment. She's fuming mad. And I suspect plotting revenge.

She keeps carrying around a little piece of paper which she *says* are her letters she's practising from school. But we've seen Kill Bill - we suspect we're on her 'list' and we'll both be sleeping with one eye open.

In a bid to try and at least pretend we still take care of ourselves, Daddy Shaun and I waxed our nose hairs the other day. It's left Daddy Shaun with a little sore cut up his nose. He says he's looked at it with a torch and, I quote, 'it looks like a tiny, new born hamster's vagina.'

Just been to my Mam's, and she loves a bargain:

'Trev, seen this clock! It was in Chiltern Mills for 4 and a half grand! Went to B&M, the EXACT same one. EXACT. SAME. ONE. 8 quid! Feel how heavy it is. Feel it. Go on. Same one.'

I just love her.

Alexis Carrington is busy writing her first novel. It's full of kicking 'k's'.

It will also contain her own illustrations. I ask what this big red thing is that she's drawn. 'Dad, it's our house. On fire.' Then she laughs. I think she's still furious about us punishing her for being naughty the other day.

At the same time, our little boy is covering my face and arms with Fireman Sam stickers then tries to pull my t shirt up, demanding 'Dad, let me see your boobies.'

Erm...'no, son. Would you mind if I don't?'

Cue; meltdown. The screams! The tears!

I hope Daddy Shaun is enjoying his first sleep in, in a week.

Packing to go on our first little family holiday to a caravan:

We've had to tell Alexis Carrington it's a luxury bungalow with an en-suite before she approved the trip.

Alexis has a whole suitcase to herself! Morning wear and evening attire for each day. Plus, shoes for every occasion you can think of. We're only going for 3 nights. She has more daily costume changes than a Cher concert. Daddy Shaun packed. The three boys have to make do with a single hold-all between us.

Little Angel Boy was dancing to the Bob the Builder theme tune and (accidentally??) farted in Alexis Carrington's face, earlier. She went green, and she started flapping her hands, wildly, whilst declaring 'that's ECUSSTING! I think I'm gonna be sick.' Then she flounced out of the room in disgust. In her Cinderella heels, of course. She probably had a conference call on her Peppa Pig mobile, anyway.

Overheard parents speaking to their kids at the caravan park soft play:

'NO Lily! At the end of the day, she's NOT your bestest friend, you'll NEVER see her again and we're going! Now MOVE! We came here to have fun as a family!!!'

Why didn't she just tell her daughter that there was no Santa, Easter Bunny or Tooth Fairy while she was at it?!

November 3 2017 ·

First week back at work done. Came home to a poorly little angel boy. House stinks of vomit. I feel green. Daddy Shaun is knackered. The dogs are past themselves dodging projectile vomit. Alexis Carrington is on form refusing to eat sausages for her tea as she's 'not in the mood.' Also, they aren't organic and the pigs weren't fed smoked salmon and M&S nibbles in their short lives, so our sausages have been branded decidedly 'council.'

Can't wait for kid's bedtime when we can get a bath. A nice relaxing bath. I might see if we have anything nice to put in the bath with me. Like an electric toaster.

November 5 2017 ·

Heating on full blast and two toddlers fresh out of pull ups fast asleep. I expect to open their bedroom door in the morning to big smiles, a stench of urine-soaked mattresses and a giant rainbow over their beds.

Actually, maybe not. They've done quite well so far.

November 11 2017 ·

Alexis Carrington had an accident at school yesterday (which wasn't her fault, and she may be entitled to compensation for.) She was pretending to be Harry Potter at school and was running in the playground using a twig she had found as a wand. She tripped over and the twig went into the corner of her eye. Her attorney is looking into it. It was quite a traumatic day for her. As soon as it happened, she cried her little eyes out, sobbing 'I am a BUPA patient - I want my own room with a TV and Tinkerbell DVD's on tap!' She has a nasty black eye but the silver lining is she gets to wear her oversized Jackie O sunglasses for a few days, so even her injury is fabulous.

It wasn't all bad news yesterday, though. She won the World Book Day competition at school too - as we climbed a local peak the other week to take a photograph of Alexis reading her favourite book, Matilda. She didn't get time to recite her acceptance speech, which had been prepared in advance, due to the accident. But it's a good job she won…otherwise… there would have been absolute hell to pay.

On a serious note, thanks everyone for the concern. She's absolutely fine, just a bit sore and bruised. She's currently getting her face painted as a tiger whilst being fed peeled grapes.

November 15 2017 ·

I just innocently pumped as I walked past Daddy Shaun to bed and I think he was furious because he said 'What an AWFUL fucking creature of a bog monster. I hope you slip away in your sleep.' He's actually mellowed since becoming a father. This is the most affectionate and flirtatious he's been towards me since we became parents. Maybe I will get lucky tonight?

November 16 2017 ·

Alexis Carrington's 5th birthday is in TWO sleeps! She's VERY excited. We have her Moana necklace wrapped up and Daddy Shaun is yet to inform me that we have actually won the lottery, which can be the only way we can afford all the stuff he's bought for this party. The Oscars was less glam.

Our tired little angel boy continues to scream and cry at anything and everything once home from nursery. He also saved a big poo for me today, which, as he was pushing it out on the toilet, he declared 'Dad, this one's fresh!' He wasn't wrong, to be fair. And I don't know when he's been eating garden peas?!

I've worked out how to deal with a tired three-and-a-half year old. Go and hide under our bed and drink wine from the bottle.

I'm so proud of my Shaun making this amazing cake for our daughter's birthday. He's spent all day on it! And it's amazing! What a labour of love. And he's saved £50 by making it himself. He's still spent thirty-four and a half THOUSAND pounds on the rest of the stuff for her party but at least we saved on the cake!!

Alexis's party speech to her guests on entrance. Tomorrow. 12pm.

'You weren't invited. I sent for you.'

I feel like that's actually fairly accurate.

Alexis Carrington approved of her day. She worked that room like Joan Collins at a champagne lunch.

She loved every minute of it.

She arrived fashionably late as she was having her hair curled. She walked hand in hand with her two dads to the entrance, with her little brother walking behind her holding her dress up so it didn't get mucky from the floor. She was slightly nervous going into a full room of mere peasants, but Daddy Shaun gave her a pep talk and she flounced in and greeted all her guests and accepted their gifts willingly.

Paw Patrol and Spider-Man made an appearance, there was soft play, a bouncy castle, a sweetie stall, face painters and a full royal banquet to feed the entire school, all of whom had turned up whether they were invited or not. This was THE party to be at and not a patch on the annual Vanity Fair Oscar Party hosted by Donatella Versace.

Alexis Carrington has arrived!

Thanks to everyone who helped out and was a part of it. Daddy Shaun did it all - I actually didn't do a thing. Except for panic, whinge and moan and clean up afterwards.

It's her actual birthday tomorrow so she gets two days to celebrate. Not like a Queen at all...

Alexis Carrington, still clearly in 'Birthday Princess' mode, has decided to up the ante in the diva behaviour. Not content with throwing a massive hissy fit at soft play yesterday (stupidly, we wanted to go home), we decided it would be lasagne for tea tonight, but we've never cooked it for her before. She struts into the kitchen after a hard day presiding over her sand pit empire, looks at it and goes 'what's that?'

When we explain it's just like flat spaghetti bolognese; she starts to lose consciousness, swooning - one hand holding herself up on the chair, the other fanning herself whilst blinking wildly; breathlessly gasping, motioning for a brown paper bag to breathe into. We rush for the smelling salts. 'Well I DON'T want that,' she asserts. She ended up eating some, throwing us hacky looks over her plate, so it wasn't all bad. She did make me a 'tendy cup of tea, which I thoroughly enjoyed, though when I asked for another one, I was curtly informed 'I'm not your slave.'

The little lad was in a surprisingly great mood after nursery today. However, after me being sick most of the day, the last thing I needed to witness was him dragging a giant greenie from his right nostril and play with it, in front of me, whilst we were sat trying to have tea at the table. I went the colour of his bogey, baulked and my tea went in the bin. He physically shuddered when he noticed the tiniest piece of red pepper hidden in his food but was quite happy to smear a giant, green bogey – freshly plucked from his right nostril - all over his plate and fork.

Oh, and the end of the meal, the pair of them looked like they'd been fed by a catapult, operated from a great distance by a partially sighted dwarf with arthritis of the hands. I have no idea how they get that messy.

November 25 2017 ·

Little lad has his finger right up his nose.

Me: 'stop picking your nose, son. Your brains will fall out.'

Him: 'Dad, where's my brains??'

Me: 'in your head.'

Him: 'Dad, let me see them. Dad, I can't see them. Dad, where are them? DAD, LET ME SEE MY BRAINNNNSS.'

Meltdown.

November 27 2017 ·

Christmas is (getting) ridiculous; having to buy everyone you know or ever met some shite they don't want or need and will never use. I have no idea what to buy that woman I passed on the M42 at high speed 6 months ago in a blue car - she looked at me, I'm sure of it, so I MUST buy her something.

Bugger it! Everyone's getting a Lynx Africa set or a box of Family Circle biscuits. The cupboard under the stairs is full of them as we were inundated with them as gifts last Christmas. So, life really is a (family) circle (of life.)

November 29 2017 ·

Alexis Carrington has been practicing her part for an Angel in her nativity. She's still absolutely fuming she didn't secure the part of Mary but all is better now she has a fiercer outfit than Mary. And wings! She kicked off because she wanted a lolly after tea and we dared to present her with a chocolate doughnut instead. She's spent some time, in tears, on the thinking step. She's made mental notes of this, and we're in her 'burn book' for sure.

The little lad is running around in his Hulk suit. Nothing much to report with him, mainly because I've managed to filter out his voice ever since he decided he would start saying 'Dad, you know..., Dad, you know... Dad, you know...' every 8 and a half seconds. Actually, I'm lying. It's every 4 and a half seconds.

December 12 2017 ·

After my little angel boy finished his Weetabix (the last in the packet) this morning, he sat in his little chair and said 'Dad, I want another one.' I replied 'I don't think we have any more, son.'

He started. 'There iiiiiiisssssssssss, in the cupboardddd.'

To avoid the morning tantrum, I get on my hands and knees with my head actually inside the cupboard and, PRAISE JESUS, I found another box of Weetabix. I rip open the box and go into stealth mode across the kitchen floor, somersault included, to get that additional Weetabix into his bowl before he goes nuclear. As I place said Weetabix delicately in his bowl with a loving 'There you go, son,' he calmly replies 'I don't want one now, Dad - I'm full!'

Well…you can imagine my buzz.

Meanwhile, after weeks of specific demands for a pink bike with compartments for jewellery and a bottle of juice, Alexis Carrington this Morning announces that she now wants a skateboard.

Game. Changer.

December 15 2017 ·

Kids are watching The Polar Express movie. They have no idea that in reality they will be on it themselves in a few hours. I am so excited - I can't waittttttttttt....

The Polar Express last night was AMAZING!

We all queued up in our pyjamas and dressing gowns and got on the train to Santa Town! We found our seats and to our horror we were all seated separately according to our tickets. The organisers came over and couldn't be more helpful and understanding and so apologetic but everywhere was full. We explained it was our first Christmas together and we really needed to be sat together, upon overhearing this, one extremely kind family with older children immediately gave up their family table so that we could all sit together and experience this together. What a kind gesture. They could see how much it meant to us and said they have done it every year with their kids so they didn't mind being seated separately. (Thank you; a million times, thank you.)

We all got cosy in our seats and the kids had hot chocolate and biscuits and danced and played games in the aisles. They had never experienced anything like this, and I'm fairly certain that they didn't really know what Christmas was, so to make their faces light up and witness that really brought a tear to our eyes. It wasn't just their first Christmas with us; it was their first every real Christmas and that thought stuck with us and made us even more determined to make this Christmas the most magical any child could ever wish for.

When the train pulled up at elf town, they both (and Daddy Shaun) squealed with excitement as they watched all the dancing elves and the Christmas lights. If they could have squeezed out of the windows to join them in a jig, I'm certain they would have.

Once we arrived back at the station, the stars were twinkling and the kids were on such a high. We carried them back to the car, and they snuggled into our shoulders and squeezed us with glee. Driving back home they were fighting sleep as they were recounting all of the magic they had just witnessed. Fairly soon though they had both passed out and I looked back at them sat it their car seats; in their dressing gowns and slippers, with blankets covering them, and I felt a rush of warmth pulse through my entire body. That's love, that is.

After the Polar Express last night, the kids had a visit from Santa and Elfie this morning and they loved it.

Alexis Carrington especially loved her gift of make-up. She's been giving me a make-over! I now look like something off Avatar auditioning for RuPaul's Drag Race. I even have ear-muffs on, and pink clips in my hair. I think she was confused when I said to 'dab' the make-up on with 'stab.' Her technique of forcefully stabbing the make-up brush deep into my pores, and soul, is very painful and she almost drew blood and took out my right eye. Bless her.

Starting our Christmas traditions as a family. All bathed; wearing new pyjamas, table set, meat in the oven, veg all prepared, Santa's mince pie and Rudolf's food put out, reindeer magic dust sprinkled on the drive to attract them. The stockings are hanging by the fireplace. The coal fire is on. We have hot chocolate in our warm mitts, we have Santa Claus: The Movie on TV. The excitement is palpable. I don't think we have ever been so happy in our lives. Soon it will be bed time for the little ones. I pray they sleep as we have a LOT to do. Merry Christmas everyone - may all your dreams come true as ours have this gorgeous year.

I'd really like us all to attend Midnight Mass one year, when the kids are older. I'm not religious, but I enjoyed the experience a few years back when Daddy Shaun and I attended a service one Christmas Eve. Even though they didn't sing any hymns we knew, such as Like a Prayer by Madonna or anything from the Sister Act movies, we still had a lovely time.

Our first Christmas as a family has been absolutely fabulous.

Daddy Shaun was the first one awake. I had to sternly advise him, as I do every year, to go back to sleep as 2am is NOT an acceptable time to get up, because Santa probably hasn't even been yet.

We crept into the kid's bedrooms at 6am — surprisingly they were still sound asleep. They clearly don't know the rules for Christmas morning; but they will get the hang of it.

We gently woke them with the sound of sleigh bells that we had rigged outside, and they both rushed to the windows in awe to discover Santa had left snow footprints all over our drive. I could have cried watching them get so excited and amazed by the whole experience. Daddy Shaun did cry. Magic is absolutely real and it was in both of their faces at that exact moment.

We all crept downstairs, whispering, as Santa may still be there. We approached our living room door with our hearts in our mouths. We discovered that Santa had stuck Christmas wrapping paper all across the doorway, and Alexis and Little Angel Boy had to smash their way through the wrapping paper to enter. They did so with the most excited squeals I have ever heard.

Their jaws hit the floor when they saw what was in front of them! Piles of presents for each of them set out and stockings overflowing.

Yes. We did spoil them and bought far too much. We just had to. We couldn't help ourselves. They deserved this!

Alexis Carrington got lots of toys and has set up a shop, a hoover (for her cleaning business), a till, a Mr Frosty and a popcorn machine. Let's just say her Empire has taken a different direction and she has fingers in many pies. She takes all major credit cards, including American Express.

The little lad got a Hulk toy and a tool box and workbench, which comes in handy after he's ran around the house screaming 'Hulk SMASH' and launched Hulk at great speed at things that can break or dent easily. He can now fix them afterwards though – by bashing the living hell out of them with his plastic hammer from his new Bob the Builder tool kit.

They also both got little keyboards and microphones and a little ukulele each. No peace can ever come of this union. The only amusing thing about these musical 'gifts,' is how they both attempt to pronounce 'ukulele.'

New Year's Resolutions:

1. Stop being fat.

2. Be thinner.

3. Delete Just Eat on January 3rd.

4. Learn to be more patient.

5. Call ambulance in advance for the Just Eat delivery driver who is running late with tonight's Chinese banquet for 6 people (though actually shared between 4 people.)

Kids are having toad in the hole for the first time for tea. Alexis Carrington will need the smelling salts to bring her round once we tell her. It's not going to go well. I feel we may just need to bribe her with cash. I haven't the strength today for the emotional tug of war and battle of wills over whether or not the sausage had a good life and what post code district it lived in before we attempt to dine.

Kids are watching Peppa Pig. Alexis Carrington is pretending she is too old to watch that now, but I see her eyeballing the screen when no one is watching. I'm googling the ages of Peppa Pig, Georgie Pig, Mummy Pig, Daddy Pig and Grandpa Pig. You'd be surprised!

This is my life now.

My little boy has watched a four-minute video of someone playing with a Spider-Man bobble head figure about a million times tonight. Is this normal? I really hope it is because I want to take him to Comic Con.

He has had me sitting with him watching it for the past 45 minutes, because – bless him – he thinks I enjoy watching it as much as he does. Over and over and over again. My face is having some sort of contraction.

We were going out for the day to the park and it was freezing. We decided to let Alexis Carrington choose her own outfit today but said it needed to be warm and with long trousers. I go upstairs and she's chosen a flouncy Princess Poppy dress. I explain she can't wear it to the park and choose her a warm tracksuit instead. She throws herself onto the bed in an Oscar worthy slow-motion dramatic style; sobbing into her pillow; it's clearly the end of her life. Anyway, we compromised on a tracksuit accessorised with a tiara for our little diva and calm descended over the household once more.

January 21 2018 ·

Kids are funny.

Alexis Carrington draws us a picture. 'Ooh, that's lovely, what is it?' I enquire. 'Fire.' She replies. I ask what's on fire. She says with glee 'Everything!'

Little lad then brings me a picture. 'Dad, this is you on fire.'

I think we'll be sleeping with the lights on, tonight. And every night from now on. Also, we must get new batteries for the smoke alarms. Also, we must buy more smoke alarms. I feel like you can never have enough.

Our kids are starting to emulate us. I just innocently pumped in front of Alexis Carrington and she sighed 'Dad, I think you need to go wipe your legs.'

Definitely our children. This is something I would say. I'd follow it up with 'I think you need to go and see a priest.'

Cuddles before bedtime; PJ's and heels! Alexis Carrington knows how to work it!

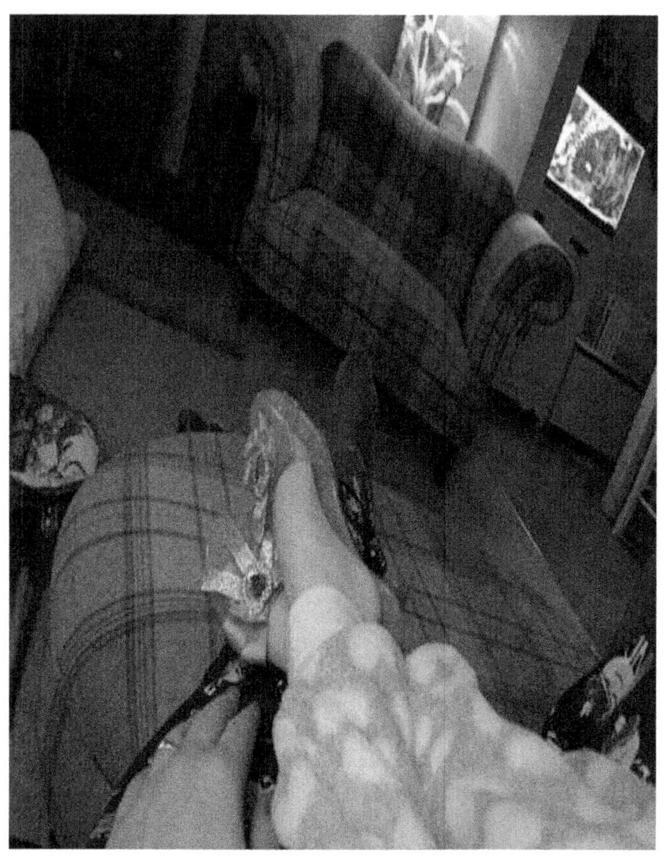

Now I'm a parent I find I have less patience. I'm more impulsive and my capacity to deal with idiots and rude people is no longer existent; which is why I am no longer allowed in Costa Coffee, where that cowbag works.

I've lost a stone since January!

Got fat again last year (had a bad weekend on the pizzas, kebabs and Ben & Jerry's) but I'm now back on the slim train.

I've been fat, I've been thin, I've been festively plump; at every size I've always been physically escorted off the premises of an all you can eat Chinese buffet, weeping silently through a mouthful of egg foo yung, with a back pack full of Tupperware.

Alexis Carrington is really into Harry Potter at the minute - it's on TV now and she just said 'look! Gary is on soon, I love Gary,'

I thought to myself, 'who the frig is Gary?'

And then he pulls up on his motorbike, full beard - and then I realise it's Hagrid she meant.

She doesn't even attempt to pronounce Hermione. She just refers to her as 'that girl.'

Alexis Carrington wants to go to sleep every night in all her fine jewellery and sunglasses etc. We have to tell her 'no' because she would come down for breakfast every day in so much gold jewellery, she would look like Mr T from the A Team.

I've now lost enough weight that when I go for a stand up wee, I can once again see my tail.

Next goal... balls.

About another stone off I reckon and they'll look massive. Like coconuts.

I was stood behind an absolute delight in B&M earlier. She was purchasing 3 bottles of wine.

She says to the cashier (who looks like Pauline Quirk, but I don't think it's actually her) 'orrrrr a love me glass a waaaarrrrrnnnn on a Fraaaaaarrrder night.'

I'm guessing it's more than a glass, sweetheart. It's likely the full THREE bottles then off to the local

Social Club to throw cans of Special Brew down your neck. Then getting scuttled behind the bins of Primark by someone in a Le Coq Sportif tracksuit, before throwing up into your kebab on the way home.

She was actually quite canny. We swapped numbers. I might see if she has any parenting tips. I do know she doesn't know how to get poo stains out of white leggings judging by her ensemble today.

March 11 2018 ·

My little amazing babies just did this for Daddy Shaun tonight, with Daddy Trev. Not that it was a surprise, as little angel boy kept coming down squealing like a girl saying "we've ran you a bath with rose petals, Dad, but shushhhhhh!! It's a surprise!" This was followed by Alexis Carrington dragging him out of the room with her hand over his mouth. It's nice for them to be a part of the Mother's Day traditions and not feel excluded - they lack for nothing! We love them both more than anything. Their little faces when I exaggerated my excitement made my heart warm.

Man, I need to lose some weight and dye my hair again. It's practically white.

Fat, gay and old. I wouldn't know what box to tick on a hate crime form...

I found a little piece of pork in my quiff tonight. Confirmed I need to get a haircut and stop being fat.

I'm calling it an 'Intervention.'

'Dad, I don't like this Twister lolly.' Said no child. Ever.

…until now!

Alexis Carrington expressed her disgust at her after dinner treat and instead requested/demanded an After Eight chocolate mint for her dessert. She probably wanted to wash it down with an Espresso or something.

It'll be Ferrero Rocher requests next.

Time Travel is possible and I can prove it.

If you want to go back to the early 1980's simply visit B&M in our local town centre at lunchtime every weekday. Specifically, it was the phase of dressing like a homeless '80's prostitute fresh out of prison. They even play Bananarama's greatest hits for that authentic desperado vibe.

You'll even bump into me, wishing I was somewhere else and tutting in the queues. Also looking like a homeless '80's prostitute fresh out of prison. Or as I like to call it 'Working Dad.'

We've just been to a water park with the kids in a bit of a rough area. Lots of crossed eyes and marijuana leaf tattoos.

Kids loved it, although Alexis Carrington declared the showers were 'hotter than the sun.'

She will be complaining in writing.

Oh, and the vending machines didn't stock Pringles or Kettle crisps; only multipack (which should not be sold separately) Golden Wonder. She's going to organise and host a benefit for those poor children who attend this water park on a regular basis.

Daddy Shaun has got the kids a duckling as a surprise for Easter. It's a surprise for them... and also me. A different kind of surprise for me. The kind of surprise like finding Hannibal Lecter is hosting Come Dine with Me and you're a guest.

We might as well sell this house and buy a fucking ark and he does need to change his name to Noah. Whatever Noah's long-suffering wife was called is what I'll change my name to.

March 24 2018 ·

I didn't even click on when I saw him Googling 'pictures of ducks.' I just assumed, as a gay man with dyslexia, he had made an ever so slight spelling mistake... (think about it. Think *harder.*)

March 25 2018 ·

I had an unsettled night's sleep last night. It was mainly due to Daddy Shaun tossing and turning because he was undecided about getting two ducklings - because he didn't want just one... in case it got lonely.

I am looking forward to us watching more of the amazing second season of our series tonight on Netflix tonight. Well I say 'us,' I mean 'me.' Shaun will be watching more videos on his phone about how to make a duckling imprint on you so you can make it think you're its mother.

I've managed to get Alexis Carrington to like Madonna and ABBA (albeit ABBA was through the Mamma Mia! movie.)

My work on Earth as a gay man is complete.

2 things my little boy told me today:

'I love you, Dad, because your hair smells nice.'

And

'Your belly is like a bouncy castle.'

He got me right in the 'feels.'

Alexis Carrington has had some teeth out and fillings today and has been very brave. She's milked it for all its worth and we've had demands for gooseberry and cinnamon yoghurt and magazines (she can't read) and she is currently writing out thank you cards for all those who have shown concern. There will be a full update in the Gazette later. Along with a photo of her looking suitably sad and swollen in her headscarf and sunglasses.

The Tooth Fairy paid a visit to Alexis Carrington last night. Alexis expected to exchange her 'naughty tooth' for shares in Chanel and the deeds to a four-bedroom Persimmon new build in an exclusive postcode, but she seemed equally buzzing with the fat penny she woke up to this morning. She has lots of plans for this shiny one- pound coin. I think disappointment will set in when she gets to Spar and realises that it won't stretch to this month's copy of Cosmopolitan.

Only joking.... Alexis won't shop at the Spar. She's a Harrods girl

The little lad and I were playing 'tendy builders at the park today. He's a proper little bloke and kept saying 'OK boss.' (I just hope and pray he doesn't ever take an interest in football. I feel sick at the thought of watching it.)

Alexis Carrington wanted to join us, until she found out she would have to *pretend* to work. She turned her nose up at the mere thought and compromised with a 'tendy job going to the 'tendy shop for 'tendy sandwiches for our 'tendy dinner.

I think she felt like shopping was a job. It's going to be an interesting chat when she leaves school. Anyway, she brought me a glass of Prosecco and sushi with a side salad with low fat dill dressing from the 'tendy shop.

Her choice, of course.

Alexis Carrington is attending 5 -year- old soft play party at 2pm.

Dressed for cocktails with Justin Beiber at 7pm. Just in case.

Werk.

Well… it's the weekend. One day I'll get a sleep in, another day I'll probably wake up at sunrise to Alexis Carrington screaming that her little angel boy brother is wiping his bum on her pillow. Or little angel boy will wake the whole house up by screaming at Alexis Carrington because she touched his Georgie Pig teddy. Or they'll both wake the whole street up because they've climbed on top of the wardrobes and launched themselves off. Or there's an argument because Alexis Carrington is demanding to play a game and wants to, obviously, be in charge. And win. Naturally, Little Angel boy has other ideas.

It's a lucky dip, really.

Sunday wake-up call was just before 7am. Screams were emanating from the bathroom because precious angel boy had sat on the toilet at the same time as Alexis Carrington and pushed her off the toilet as she was mid poo. She's stood with a turtle's head, devastated, while he goes about his business.

Hell. On.

I decide to walk them to my Mam's which is a 20-minute walk through fields and woods. An HOUR later we finally arrive at Nanny's. It took that long because they had to stop and shout 'Dad, Dad, DAAADDD, watch this!' every 7 and a half seconds of our journey. I'm thinking about changing my name to something they seem to have great difficulty pronouncing. Like 'please' or 'thank you.'

Also, I didn't realise how sore your throat can get by saying 'oh wow that's AMAZING,' each time the kids tell you to watch them do a big jump, which in all fairness, are probably the smallest jumps in the universe. Bless them.

April 15 2018 ·

Gave the kids a chocolate yoghurt for dessert. The little lad comes over when he's finished and looks like he's had a mud bath. Whilst I'm cleaning him up, I ask how, on EARTH, does he have chocolate up to both his elbows?

His response? 'I was licking my arms, Dad.'

Fair enough.

We got the kids a ukulele each for Christmas. They're both showing a real talent for music, though it turns out that the little lad might just be more of a drummer. How do we know this? Because he decided do bash his ukulele over Alexis Carrington's head as if it were a tennis ball. Seems he wants to hit something with something else so maybe drumming is his forte. Or tennis.

Alexis Carrington wasn't badly injured, though she did remind us, as she swooned and held on to her chest with one hand and the arm of the sofa with the other, that should she ever need hospital treatment that she was a BUPA person and she expects a private room with Barbie cartoons on demand and Sugar Puffs served in a glass slipper for breakfast.

I just gave Alexis Carrington a Peppa Pig yoghurt as her dessert.

And she gave me a look that suggested she thought I was trying to harvest her organs.

I don't want your spleen, sweetheart, Dad's just trying to give you a nice, healthy dessert.

We had to take Alexis Carrington to the doctors tonight as she was looking a bit flushed and red in the face. Turns out she has an ailment that's actually called 'Slap Face.' We're assured by Alexis that she hasn't been involved in any cat fights with Crystal Carrington in the playground. Turns out it's a viral thing that will clear up in a few days. CUE Alexis' sad face and poorly voice the SECOND the doctor made a diagnosis. This is after she skipped into his office in her pink princess heels.

While the doctor was checking her over, he pointed out she had something lodged inside her ear! We all had a look and it was round and green, suspiciously Smartie-esque, and what's more- Alexis didn't know it was there or how it got there or what it is - so the mystery object will be removed in hospital on Monday.

No-one knows how long it's been stuck in there and Alexis claims to have no recollection of putting anything in there.

It's certainly never affected her hearing as she can hear a Kinder Egg being unwrapped from 300 yards away. She has bat-like hearing and you only have to whisper the words 'Chanel Couture' and she's there with her unicorn purse wanting a donation to her fashion cause.

In other Alexis news, she has recovered from her brother hitting her around her head with his ukulele, and she has been in touch with her legal representation to discuss a claim for an accident that wasn't her fault, and for which she may be due compensation. Allegedly. Her brother has declined to comment and remains unbothered.

April 21 2018 ·

Alexis Carrington had her tap dance exam this morning. Sunglasses were a MUST. To avoid the paparazzi, obviously.

April 23 2018 ·

Meltdown with a 3-year-old on a dog walk. 'DAD THERE'S SOMETHING IN MY SHOEEEE!!'

'Don't worry, son, it's probably just a little stone,' I explain.

'IT'S NOTTTTT' he screams back with real tears in his eyes.

'OK, it's a bit of soil.' I say, tearing his shoe off before four horsemen appear over the hill and the skies turn blood red.

'NOOOOOOO!!!!' He's actually full-on screaming at this point!

'Ok, it's probably an elephant in your sock.' I say, knowing the sarcasm in my tone will be completely lost...

'Yeah it is, Dad, except it's a tiger.' He calmly responds, no tears, happy in the realisation I finally discovered what was in his sock - because I'm too stupid to realise it was an elephant tiger in the first place.

Problem solved.

Until... I ask him to put his shoe back on. That's when the pits of hell rip open wide and I can actually feel the heat of Satan's sweet breath on the back of my neck.

Alexis Carrington had her hair done by Daddy Trev this morning. I did my first ponytail and was so proud of myself! Alexis noted my efforts and will pass comment on them at my monthly parenting appraisal next week which she will chair and advise me on areas of improvement.

The little lad saw my delight and wanted a ponytail too. He had a meltdown because it wasn't like his sister's. Silly Daddy Trev not having the ability to make human hair grow to a desired length instantly. Must do better.

Just tucked the kids in bed. Little lad is snuggled up with his Georgie Pig and Hulk teddies.

Alexis Carrington snuggled up with her new handbag and bottle of perfume.

I'm not even joking.

When the kids shriek the name 'DAAAAADD' (which is constantly,) I'm not going to respond with 'what?' anymore.

Instead, I'm going to reply with 'Did you rub the lamp, master?'

Now that she has passed her tap dancing exam and is considered an accomplished dancer, when asked if she enjoyed her cordon bleu dinner of fish fingers and chips this evening, instead of replying verbally, Alexis Carrington decided she would perform an interpretive dance regarding her evening culinary experience.

Judging by the scrunched-up pout and jerky hand gestures, I'm going to assume it was a hit!

We just need to find a way to break it to her that it's lasagne for tea tomorrow night. She needs to be gently prepared for 'foreign food.'

May 3 2018 ·

Exactly one year ago today, at 3 o'clock in the afternoon, Shaun and I had just arrived at our hotel on holiday in Turkey when we received a call from our Adoption Social Worker. After months of set-backs and reports, and ups and downs, it was finally agreed that everyone was happy for us to be put forward as potential fathers to our little girl and boy.

Exactly one year later, at half 10 this morning, after months of set-backs and reports, and ups and downs, we received another call from our Adoption Social Worker to say that FINALLY, some judges in a courtroom have at last granted a full adoption order and we are now legal parents of our little girl and boy.

It's mad how things work out. 12 months to the day.

Alexis Carrington is over the moon she finally gets a double-barrelled surname and her playground social status is at last cemented.

Our little angel boy doesn't really care as he doesn't see the difference, because despite what we tell him, he maintains that he came from Daddy Shaun's tummy and that his life started when we met him as far as he's concerned. And do you know what? If that makes him happy, then we're all cool with that.

We are now a legally recognised family.

What a journey!

May 5 2018 ·

Paddling pool in the garden for the kids today as it's a scorcher!

Alexis Carrington is sprawled out in her finest bikini and Chanel goggles, making various demands without blinking: 'Get me a drink! Get me a snack! Get me my little unicorn bath toy!'

She's also complained that the paddling pool is a tad too cold for her liking so Daddy Shaun has dismantled the plumbing under the sink as the hose pipe won't fit on the tap in the house, only the outside tap. He has re-plumbed the entire sink underneath and turned up the heat on the boiler to maximum and refilled the paddling pool with hot water to appease her.

All was well until Little Angel boy decided to squirt her full force in the face with his Fireman Sam Super Soaker. Absolute hell on.

She wants a hot tub and a little sister, pronto!

Most of my day has been spent repeating the same phrase over and over again like a mantra:

'STOP holding your sister's head under the water until the bubbles stop, son.'

Alexis Carrington and her representatives have been approached for comment, but have yet to release an official statement.

I can confirm that she is currently in her pink PJ's and princess heels, on her fur blanket; nibbling a humble After Eight mint chocolate for movie night whilst getting some lovely Daddy cuddles.

They've both got the exact same breakfast cereal spoon, but he's furious that Alexis Carrington won't let him touch her spoon.

Note the poo emoji teddy he simply had to bring to breakfast just to annoy Alexis. (Her heartfelt pleas of 'Dad, that poo makes me feel sick!!! echoing around the dining room.)

No. I don't miss my Sunday morning sleep-in followed by a leisurely potter around a (quiet) house, casually getting ready for the day at my own pace. At all. Not one bit.

PS. Sometimes I lie.

Daddy Shaun and I had long suspected Alexis Carrington was the culprit responsible for waking Little Angel Boy up every morning by going over to his bed and whispering to him so we wouldn't hear her wake him up. The reason she does this is because she's an early riser and she's astute enough to know that once Little Angel Boy is awake – then so is everyone else in this house and in our street. He can't whisper. He can't play quietly. He can't do anything quietly.

When we approached Alexis about our suspicions, she came clean and admitted that she woke him up every morning because she was bored and wanted us to get all to get up. She is a busy lady, you see, and she has places to go and people to see. She agreed that instead of waking Little Angel Boy up every morning, she would lay quietly in her bed and play with her teddies and skim through her books and the latest copy of Hello magazine until it was time to get up for breakfast.

Daddy Shaun and I thought this would mean that instead of waking up to the sound of all hell breaking loose in the next room every morning; with little, sticky handprints on the ceiling and Little Angel Boy deciding to break into a morning chorus of Old McDonald had a farm (but zero sleep, apparently) in the loudest, deepest, shout-y voice a 3 year old boy can muster at 6.30am, we would instead have the opportunity to rise before our children and wake them up gently with a warm flannel over their forehead and whispering gently to stir them awake nicely.

Alexis Carrington, on the other hand, was hatching a different plan.

Ever since our chat with her, she has kept to her word about not going over to her little brother's bed each morning and shaking him awake. Instead, now, every morning at around 6am, Alexis develops a nasty, loud, throaty, forced fake cough, which only ever seems to ail her at 6am and seems to ease off once Little Angel Boy is swinging from the light shade shouting his ABC's at full decibel. He also likes to stamp - VERY loudly - pretending to be some kind of large dinosaur trying to smash his way through the floor into the kitchen below. Or at least that's our impression.

So, nothing has changed in our house with our morning routine. Except Alexis is now fully blameless and sits with an innocent look on her face. Halo firmly intact above her head.

Little Angel Boy has his 4th birthday party tomorrow, which is Super Hero themed. He's been waiting all week and is so super excited!

We let him try on his new Captain America outfit on tonight because he's been absolutely BURSTING to see it. He wants to sleep in it tomorrow night. We're currently mentally preparing ourselves for the mental breakdown at bedtime tomorrow if this doesn't happen.

Not to be left out, we also bought Alexis Carrington a Spider-Girl outfit so she could swish about the house and feel special too.

We decided to take a photograph of the cuteness overload.

Soon after the taking of this photograph, Alexis Carrington threw a massive hissy fit; real tears and everything. Sobbing, she was. The reason? She realised she didn't have the correct footwear to match her outfit.

Her wardrobe (which could house a small family of dwarves it's that big) was turned inside out whilst she frantically searched for the right style of shoe. Alas, she just didn't have anything she liked. In the end she plumped for the old faithful's; the plastic, pink princess heels. They don't go with the outfit one bit.

But, Jesus Christ, no one in this is going to mention a thing and bring that fact to her attention.

Little Angel Boy uttered the words we both just couldn't wait to hear tonight.

'Dad, I want to go to football.'

Well, that's fine, because I'll be dragging him to Madonna concerts and the Eurovision Song Contest finals, so we will even out the balance.

Alexis Carrington reluctantly agreed to try a yellow pepper tonight. She took the tiniest nibble of the end and then proceeded to take 4 and a half minutes to chew and swallow the offending vegetable. She looked like she was going to burst into tears at several points during this cruel torture…but at least she tried. We told her we were very proud of her trying new food. She looked very pleased with her accomplished self. She then asked for a Mercedes for her good behaviour.

We did take Little Angel Boy to football and he absolutely loves it. He goes once a week, though seems to enjoy picking the ball up and running away with it when someone else manages to tackle it away from him.

Little Angel Boy on a dog walk:

Him: 'Dad, carry meeeeeeee!!!'

Me: 'I'm not carrying you, son. You can walk; you're a big boy!'

Him: 'Dad, give me a hug.'

I pick him up and give him a massive hug.

Whilst in my arms, mid-hug, he looks in my eyes and smiles and says: 'Now walk.'

Clever.

Daddy Shaun and I had our first proper night out (out) since we became Dads. Nanna Mushroom came to stay over to look after Alexis Carrington and Little Angel Boy, and they had a great time with sweets and popcorn.

Nanna Mushroom even got up early with them and took them out for the day on the bus to her house so Dads could have a sleep in!

The kids loved their bus ride, though Little Angel Boy was annoyed that he wasn't allowed to press the 'STOP' bell constantly for half an hour or hang from the windows while the bus was moving. Alexis Carrington enjoyed herself too, although she commented that the smell of mere peasant was a tad overpowering on her bus journey that morning. I told her she will get used to it, but until she does, she should always keep a bottle of Chanel with her to spray directly into the peasant's direction. She agreed this was a suitable solution and the risk assessment was signed off.

May 25 2018 ·

It's the final day of the kids' Sports Week (a full week no less) at school and nursery today.

As they've been worn out all week, Daddy Shaun got up extra early to cook a nice breakfast of beans, eggs, toast, bacon and mushrooms for our little dears. They usually have cereal, but they've done so well this week and we wanted them to be ready for the final day. As he's busying away downstairs, before a full hard day of graft at work himself, I go and wake the kids up with a lovely smile and a 'Good Morning!'

They rub their eyes, smiling away at me. Alexis Carrington enquires what the smell is. I tell them that

Daddy Shaun is cooking a nice big breakfast before they do their race at school.

Alexis Carrington's face plummeted. 'Oh, no. Oh, no!,' she asserts. 'I'm not having bacon. I want cereal.'

Now, she likes bacon. She likes toast. She likes beans. She's indifferent to eggs and she hates mushrooms (though doesn't seem to notice when I grate them into tiny pieces in stews and her favourite Bolognese sauce.)

I tell her she can have cereal too, but Daddy Shaun wanted to do something special for them so they were big and strong for their day ahead.

Her lips pursed. Her pupils fully dilated to saucer size. Her eyes narrowed. Her nose scrunched up. And the hands went firmly to her hips. 'I DON'T WANT BACON.'

I back out of the room slowly, like a meer-kat faced with an angry lion on the Serengeti. I try not to look directly at her. I bow my head in submission and quickly escape her 'glare.' It's time for Little Angel Boy and I to make a run for it downstairs.

He sits and the table, buzzing with his little life because he will eat ANYTHING; Any food, any sweet, any crayon. He sits singing away to us with a slice of crispy bacon in each hand; beans on the ceiling – our Barker & Stonehouse dining room table now translucent with greasy hand (and foot!) prints! Alexis Carrington cautiously creeps downstairs to join us and perches herself at the table; half huffily; half sheepishly.

She sees how hard Daddy Shaun has worked on the presentation and gives a nod of semi-approval. Then she reels off a list of what's on the plate that she will not be eating (mushrooms and eggs.) Then she tucks in.

Maybe we should stick to madam's continental breakfast of cured meats and pain au chocolat from now on. Clearly the full English is far too working class for Alexis.

May 25 2018

I took Little Angel Boy to bed early tonight as he was tired and working his ticket. We read 'The Tiger Who Came to Tea' for the 16th night in a row. He had a meltdown over me not letting him sleep in his cowboy hat and with his tape measure. He's measured me 26 and a half THOUSAND times tonight. Apparently, according to his measurements, I'm '5 to 8,' which is a... revelation.

Alexis Carrington spent quiet time getting cuddles off Daddy Shaun as she was a bit teary tonight. Mainly because she was offered a bacon sandwich for breakfast this morning instead of her usual espresso and croissant, and she still hasn't quite gotten over the ordeal. We have explained that this wasn't prison food and that we eat bacon sandwiches when we're skint like poor people do. She started to hyperventilate when she heard the word 'skint' but we reassured her that it was payday today and that her Special K would be back on the menu tomorrow. She went to bed clutching her jewels.

May 27 2018 ·

This morning I asked Little Angel Boy to sit on the sofa next to his sister, quietly, while I got ready upstairs.

His response? 'But Dad, I don't like her breath.'

To be fair, Alexis Carrington does have stinky morning breath. She just threw him a casual glance which suggested she was about to say: 'bore someone else with your problems, darling,' but she didn't. It was the only time I have felt disappointment in her abilities to destroy someone with a withering comment.

Thoughts for the day from my children:

Alexis Carrington: 'I can't fit under the chair, Dad, 'cause I've got a big, massive, big, fat head.'

Little Angel Boy: 'Dad, my mouth just pumped.'

Praise be for bedtime!

Trying to play a game of Word Association (Mallet's Mallet; without the mallet) with the kids and, Jesus WEPT, it was hard work.

Daddy Shaun chooses the word 'mouse.'

Little Angel Boy: 'food!'

Daddy Shaun: 'why food????'

Little Angel Boy: 'cause mice eat food, Dad.'

Daddy Shaun: *sigh* 'Fair enough, right, Lex, your word is food... go!'

Alexis Carrington: 'Blood!!!'

Maybe Alexis was thinking outside of the box and associated vampires with food, or maybe she could see the blood trickling from Daddy Shaun and Daddy Trev's ears. It's not a game we'll be playing again in a hurry as it just sends the stress levels through the roof. My face had a contraction at one point. Blood pressure is soaring.

May 31 2018 ·

Alexis Carrington can't pass up a chance to poo in someone else's toilet. She was in Pizza Hut today, nibbling a humble crust of deep pan margherita when she felt a bit bubbly.

I take her to the toilet and as she squeezes ferociously on the pot, she informs me that every time she does a poo; she cries! That's right! Every time she squashes a frog; water comes out of her eyes, apparently. I said it's probably because she's pushing her poo out too hard. Now, She can wipe her own bum, but I happened to catch sight of what she had passed as she ascended the throne, and I can tell you, it made MY eyes water looking at the size of it, winking back at me from its Saniflow water nest. It was something a fully grown 7-foot bloke would be proud of the morning after a king-sized mixed grill and a few pints after the footie.

If that washes up on the beach, she will have folk questioning whether or not it's some new species of giant sea mammal.

I asked her if it hurt her when she went for a poo, because as a parent – I need to know whether or not my Princess needs a stool softener or more fibre, but she advised me that it doesn't hurt and that she likes going for a poo. Her eyes just water. Definitely my daughter!

Bless her.

June 3 2018 ·

The transformation of our house into an Ark continues...

We are now the proud owners of a hamster.

Little Angel Boy keeps calling it a mouse.

Little Angel Boy also believes that one day he will become a mouse and when he does, he asked if he can play on our mouse's slide. I explained, for the fifth time, that it's not a mouse, it doesn't have a slide on his cage; that's a tunnel, and that unfortunately when Little Angel Boy grows up, he won't become a mouse, or any other animal. Little Angel Boy's response to my earth-shattering revelations?

'Ok, Dad. But when I'm older and I'm a mouse, can I go on this slide? And when you grow up and you're a mouse, you can go on this slide, can't you, Dad?'

I've just gone along with it...

June 9 2018 ·

Daddy Shaun worked very hard yesterday to split the kid's bedrooms up, as it was time they had their own space for their toys and clothes. Little Angel Boy got his first big boy bed and Alexis Carrington now has space for her board meetings, manicures and cartwheels.

To celebrate, we also let them for the first time choose their own after dinner treat and let them go into the cupboard and pick one thing from the chocolate basket. Alexis picked her trusty mint chocolates and Little Angel Boy grabbed a tin of Ambrosia Devon custard instead - because it was the biggest thing in the cupboard.

Then, at bedtime, they went in their own rooms- super excited- and went to sleep quickly. It was the first time they had ever not slept in the same room. So far - so good.

This morning, we woke to discover a number of 'firsts' for Little Angel Boy. He had woken up this morning, decided for the first time ever to come downstairs on his own and get into the chocolate basket in the cupboard and fill his little hamster pouches with all the chocolate he could find. Then he decides to stumble upstairs, half in a Cadbury induced coma, with fists full of mini snack size Chunky Kit Kats and Rocky Robins and he leaps onto Alexis Carrington in her sleep, and proceeds to shower her with chocolate coins as he's decided to have a party. We were rudely awoken by the sounds of screams due to hair pulling and general chaos.

I was furious! I sat Little Angel Boy down and told him how disappointed I was that he came downstairs to raid the sweetie cupboard and that he should never, EVER do that again without first waking me up as it's very, VERY inconsiderate to have a midnight feast without fat dad. I also pointed out where the Pringles were kept for his next expedition.

Mission: catch Little Angel Boy pinching chocolate when we're all asleep.

Method: setting the downstairs burglar alarm and pointing the sensor at mischievous 4-year-old height.

Alternative method considered: baby gate at top of landing. Method rejected on the grounds of mischievous 4-year-old being a master of escape and stealthy as fuck.

Outcome: when the alarms go off, he'll shit himself and never do it again.

Source: Crystal ball.

To his credit, Little Angel Boy has never repeated The Great Chocolate Heist of 2018 (that we have ever discovered evidence of, anyway.)

Took the kids to town today to buy Daddy Shaun's first Father's Day presents.

I hope he enjoys a multipack of 7 Snickers (Little Angel Boy's choice,) and a My Little Pony notebook and pen (Alexis Carrington's choice.)

They were both adamant that these are the gifts Daddy Shaun really wants and needs.

I intervened and we bought other things. I told the kids not to tell Daddy Shaun what we bought as it's a surprise. As soon as we got home, Little Angel Boy runs straight over to Daddy Shaun all excited, and shouts 'Dad, we bought you a cup and chocolates, but I'm not supposed to say 'cause it's a surprise. Ok, Dad?' Those were literally the first words he bellowed as soon as we got home. It was like he was going to burst unless he told Daddy Shaun.

Alexis Carrington has gone political! The council (a word that Alexis gags at when she attempts to pronounce it, as it has associations of the Shameless estate and home-made tattoo's and last season Primark fashion,) have put forward plans to build houses on a meadow near our house where we walk our dogs every night. She has heard Daddy Shaun and I talking about it and knows that we are involved in a protest against it. She took it upon herself to write the 'naughty council' a letter of her own: 'I am so sad. No houses to build. I am Alexis. Angel Boy, Dad, Dad, Fluffy' (our tortoise.)

She makes us proud everyday just by being a strong little girl, but this was a huge surprise as she did it unprompted and without any help. We couldn't be prouder that her efforts have made the news; Twitter and a magazine. It won't be the last of her strongly worded letters, I'm sure. We're both such super-proud parents to have such a caring little girl, who let's not forget is only 5 years old.

Alexis has spoken. Let her voice be heard. She will strike fear into the hearts of all the naughty council men and women who want to build on her meadow!

Best of all – it worked!!! The council eventually abandoned their plans to build. Alexis wins again! She now says she wants to don her Spider-Girl outfit and go out at night and fight crime.

June 14 2018 ·

Little Angel Boy just tried to kick me.

Alexis Carrington looked shocked and appalled at him and said 'that's illegal. Don't kick Dad.'

Bad laughing. She's not wrong, though.

June 18 2018 ·

It seems Alexis Carrington has learned a new word.

We all sat down to eat our tea tonight. It was something we don't have very often – beef stew!

Alexis Carrington looks at it in mild disgust as it is delicately placed in front of her and she cautiously starts to spoon it into her mouth. When we had it before, she declared it was simply 'delicious' and that Daddy Trev was 'the best cook in the world,' so we didn't think we would have to mentally 'prepare' Alexis for this particular meal tonight.

We can see her picking out the vegetables and avoiding the rest.

I glance over at her and say she needs to eat it all up so she can grow big and strong.

She just stares blankly at me. I can see a battle of wills about to commence.

I joke with her 'if you don't eat it all up – I'm going to tip what's left in the bowl over your head.'

She puts down her spoon, leans back in her chair with her hands casually placed behind her head (which has been adorned by a dazzling blue tiara for tonight's meal) and she calmly exclaims 'well….that's illegal.'

Today she has clearly been in counsel with her legal representation.

Alexis 1 – Daddy Trev NIL.

September 27 2018

Me: 'What did you have for dinner today at school, son?'

Little Angel Boy: 'not beans.'

Me: 'You didn't have beans?'

Little Angel Boy: 'No, I didn't have beans.'

Me: 'So what DID you have for dinner?'

Little Angel Boy (highly annoyed): 'I just told you! Not beans.'

Me: **sigh** **turns to Alexis Carrington** 'So, what did you have for dinner then, Princess?'

Alexis Carrington: 'Beans.'

Little Angel Boy then farts, whilst sat on my knee, and it's a full-on nuclear stinker.

Someone is lying about beans!

September 29 2018 ·

My little boy just said the sweetest thing to me as he gave me a big cuddle:

'Dad, you smell like bacon.'

The kids wanted to play I Spy around the breakfast table this morning. I don't particularly value my sanity; so I agreed - since they both now know at least some letters.

I pick M for mirror.

Little Angel Boy: 'is it Dad?'

Me: 'No. That begins with D.'

Little Angel Boy: 'OK. Is it Apple?'

Me: 'No. That begins with A. And we don't have any apples. We have pears in the fruit bowl.'

Little Angel Boy: 'Pear!'

Me: 'No, son. That begins with P. We're looking for letter M.'

Little Angel Boy: 'Fish tank!'

Me: 'No. That's an F.'

Alexis Carrington: 'Monkey!'

Me: 'No. Where is there a monkey in this room??'

Alexis Carrington: 'OK, I give up.'

Little Angel Boy: 'My turn!!! I spy with my little eye something beginning with cat.'

Me: 'OK. We don't have a cat. We can't see a cat. And you need to say the letter. So, if it's 'wall' you see then you begin with the letter W. Ok? Try again.'

Little Angel Boy: 'OK, I spy with my little eye something beginning with W.'

Me: 'Oh, I don't know, could it by any chance be wall???'

Little Angel Boy (very excited): 'Yes, Dad. It's your turn now because you got that one.'

Alexis Carrington (fuming): 'No! I haven't had a turn!!'

Me: 'Alright. You have a turn first.'

Alexis Carrington (smug): 'I spy with my little eye something beginning with O.'

Me: 'This is a hard one. I can't see anything beginning with O. Is it orange? Because I can see an orange crayon.'

Alexis Carrington looks around the room frantically and I can see her little brain on overload: 'No. That's not it.'

Me: 'You can't see anything beginning with O, can you? You're trying to find something now, aren't you?'

Alexis Carrington: 'Nooo! I can see something beginning with O.'

Me: 'OK, smartypants, what is it then?'

Alexis Carrington sits in silence; half smiling: 'ermmmm.... your turn.'

Me: 'I spy with my little eye something beginning with S.'

Little Angel Boy: 'Orange!!'

Alexis Carrington: 'Snake!!'

Me: **sigh** 'where is there a snake in this room????'

S also stands for simpleton.

Hurry up and get up Daddy Shaun!!!

Alexis Carrington is over the moon - she tried a new food at school today! As she's a fussy little bugger, we tear our hair out trying to get her to try new food.

Alexis (bursting with excitement): 'Dad!! I tried something new at school today!'

Me: 'oh wow! Well done! What did you try??'

Alexis (eyes sparkling with pride): 'egg and tuna!!'

Me: 'that's fab! Did you like it?'

Alexis: 'not exactly.'

Me: 'Why? Didn't you like the taste?'

Alexis: 'I didn't taste it. I went up to it and smelled it and said 'NO.' Are you proud of me?'

Me: 'yes, sweetheart.'

Alexis (chuffed): 'I gonna try something new tomorrow, too.'

Everybody has heard of Martin Lewis' Money Saving Expert tips. Well, let me tell you about Daddy Shaun's money wasting tips. On a balmy October night of 12 degrees, he decided to turn up the heating to MAX and inform me that he had only put it on timer to come on for an hour during the night. I woke up for a wee at 2am in a pool of my own sweat. I crawled across the landing, parched, desperate to be rehydrated by a few drips of water from the tap in the bathroom. I enter the bathroom, which now feels like the inside of Mount Vesuvius, moments before it erupted, and pass by the radiator. As my bare leg brushes past it, I am scorched by said radiator which is now so hot that the paint has started to blister, and I fall to the fall, writing in pain with 3rd degree burns. The bowels of hell have seen milder climes.

I look in on the kids, who thankfully have never had an accident during the night, otherwise I would have expected a rainbow to have appeared over their beds. I look at the boiler and Daddy Shaun has put the wrong setting on and instead of it being on timer, it is on constant. I can't wait for the next gas bill.

October 27 2018 ·

The clocks go back tonight. I'm really looking forward to my extra hour of Power Rangers and listening to a four and five-year-old whine 'Daaaa-aaaad, he's looking at meeeee!' or 'Daaaaa-aaaad, she's touching my teddy,' for another hour. It's my absolute favourite.

We introduced The Goonies to the kids tonight. Here's a little insight of how we watched the movie with 4 year old Little Angel Boy:

Him: 'Dad, who's that?'
Me: 'Chunk'
Him: 'who's Chunk?'
Me: 'Him on the telly, there!'
Him: 'Dad, what's Chunk doing?'
Me: 'Helping Sloth.'
Him: 'Dad, who's Sloth?'
Me: 'Him on the telly, there!'
Him: 'Dad, what's Sloth doing?'
Me: 'he's going to help Chunk and The Goonies'
Him: 'Dad, who are the Goonies?'
Me: 'All those kids on the telly, there!!'
Him: 'Dad, what are The Goonies doing?'
Me: 'Looking for One Eyed Willie's treasure.'
Him: 'who's One Eyed Willy?'
Me: 'The Pirate.'
Him: 'Dad, where's Chunk and Sloth?'
Me: 'they're coming soon - they're after the bad guys.'
Him: 'Dad, who are the bad guys?'
Him: 'Dad, why is Sloth Superman now?'
Me: 'He's not he's just got a Superman t shirt on.'

Him: 'Why, Dad?'
Me: 'because he likes Superman.'
Him: 'i like Superman too, don't I, Dad?'
Me: 'yes you do, son'
Him: 'Dad, where did his t shirt come from?'
Me: 'the shop?'
Him: 'which shop, Dad?'

And so on and so forth...

How he hasn't lost his voice I just don't know. My nerves are in pieces.

October 28 2018 ·

Take away delivery late!

Not being funny but I hope there's a Priest following the delivery driver because he'll need his last rites after I've finished with him once the food arrives.

Never keep a fat man on the cusp of malnutrition! I've only had one tiny little Pizza Hut buffet today.

Beaming with pride after Parent's Evening:

Alexis Carrington is one of the brightest in her class. At 5 years old she has single-handedly devised a business plan for the school where it will save £1.2 billion in the next fiscal year. She did a power point presentation on her Tomy Etch-a-Sketch and is nominated for Business Woman of the Year at the CBeebies Dragon's Den Awards. She is also potentially on the New Year's Honours list for services to fashion. She made gold and black polka dot tutus and My Little Pony sparkly gem encrusted notepads THE must-have ensemble in the playground this year.

Little Angel Boy did equally as well. A gifted artist (with the creative temperament to match,) he erected scaffolding in the school gym one lunch hour, and recreated the ceiling of the Sistine Chapel with his own fair hands and a pack of pastel Crayola crayons without any help. His charity work with underprivileged trainee 'tendy Power Rangers has won the hearts of his teachers and he has had the nod that his Batman role play acting and tantrums will win him the Nobel Prize for drama this year. And a Bafta.

So proud of our babies.

'Poo' seems to be THE most hysterically funny word and the topic of EVERY conversation when you're 4 and 5 years old.

If the conversation doesn't start about poo; it sure ends as one.

Also - making fart noises every 6 and a half seconds is apparently a thing.

Movie night. The kids are allowed pizza and sweets, watching a movie on their blanket.

Little Angel Boy has just stood up and farted in Alexis Carrington's face just as she had taken a bite of her margherita. The beast was then unleashed out of its cage. Tears were forming as she whimpered 'Daaaaaddddd, he's just pumped in my face and put me off my pizza.'

Little Angel Boy has been told to leave the room if he needs to pump while they're having their tea. He's currently out of the room – pumping - and giggling! To be fair I feel like joining him.

Little Angel Boy has been pushing his luck lately.

Last night, Daddy Shaun had a headache and went to bed after tea for half an hour. Ten minutes after Daddy Shaun had gone up the stairs, Little Angel Boy declares that he needs a wee. I tell him to go to the toilet but be quiet so he doesn't wake Daddy Shaun up. He says 'OK, Dad!' and disappears off up the stairs. 3 seconds later, from upstairs, I can hear Little Angel Boy shouting 'Dad! Dad!' - as if to rouse someone. I dash upstairs faster than a fat man going for the last Cantonese spare rib at an all you can eat Chinese Buffet. Sure enough, there's Little Angel Boy in our bedroom, stood bedside our bed, trying to wake Daddy Shaun up. In my angriest whisper I say 'get into the bathroom, have you wee and leave Daddy Shaun sleep!!' He toddles off to the toilet and sits there having his wee. Using my angry whisper, I say 'why did you try and wake Daddy Shaun up when you said you needed a wee and I asked you to be quiet???' He looks at me, puts his finger to his lips and goes 'SSSHHHHH!!! You'll wake Daddy Shaun up!' I just had to leave the room and count to ten; my face looks like a new born hamster with Bell's Palsy and I'm frothing at the mouth with an uncontrollable twitch in my right eye

Then, this morning, for the first time ever, I sleep in for work. I frantically leap out of bed and get washed and dressed then get the kids up and make their beds and we make our way downstairs. I ask them both if they've been to the toilet and they both say 'yes, Dad.'

The second we sit down at the breakfast table, Little Angel Boy announces that he needs a poo. Off he goes upstairs. I tell him I'll be up to help him wipe his bum when I've combed my hair and put my shoes on. It takes about a minute comb my hair and put my shoes on and then as I get to the bottom of the stairs, I find Little Angel Boy stood there. He immediately informs me he's wiped his own bum. I tell him to go back upstairs as I need to check his bum to make sure he's done it properly, as I know his version of 'clean' is to waft the toilet paper around his backside once after a poo, and then let his Avengers undies do the work of real superheroes. He throws himself in an ever so dramatic fashion, face-down on the stairs and screams 'I HAVEEEEEE!' My patience this morning is like an elastic band that has been stretched to capacity so I say nothing and just pick him up and take him upstairs. Upon checking I see he didn't wipe his bum properly, he didn't flush the chain, and he didn't wash his hands. He did however manage to smear poo all over the toilet seat and his pyjama bottoms and his hands and everything he touched on his way downstairs. I arrive back down the stairs to a written formal complaint from Alexis Carrington who apparently has been given the wrong spoon to eat her cereal with this good morning. She's tapping her foot and offering the spoon back to Daddy Trev, who is now lobster red and sweating profusely and REALLY late for work. Little Angel Boy follows behind me singing some inane little tune perforated with blowing raspberry sounds to emulate a fart noise. What a time to be alive!

Alexis Carrington has just said her first swear word.

Alexis: 'Dad, can I have a crap, please?'

Daddy Shaun: 'Excuse me?! What did you just say?'

Alexis (in a confused and slightly hesitant voice): 'I want a crap,' she reiterates, motioning towards the cupboard.

Daddy Shaun: 'Ahhhhh......you want a CREPE??' as he holds an actual crepe in his hand.

Daddy Shaun explained to her that 'crap' is a swear word. Alexis immediately requests the presence of her solicitor. She went onto explain it was a simple mistake and she will not be judged based on her innocent mistake and that there will be no disciplinary repercussions from her faux pas as it's not her fault.

Her face was a picture when she realised she had used a naughty word. However - her brother continued to repeat 'CREPE!, CRAP!, CREPE!, CRAP!'

continuously in the background – even making up a little tune to sing the words along to, which was a treat for us all. Funnily enough, whenever he burps, he can't seem to remember the word 'pardon.' When he does accidentally hear a naughty word, it seems to imprint on his soul immediately and forever.

Alexis has apologised profusely at least 52 times in the past ten minutes.

Little Angel Boy continues on his cheeky path.

I was tucking him into bed tonight and I said to him 'you're my favourite little boy in the whole world!'

With a big, cheeky smile, he snaps back with 'I am, aren't I, darl?'

I chuckle to myself and kiss him goodnight and say 'love you, son.'

His reply is (affecting a cheesy American accent) 'love you, babes!'

Little Angel Boy has been given the part of Joseph in his school Nativity.

When Daddy Shaun found out he was in floods of tears in the playground.

I can imagine, given Little Angel Boy's current personality quirks, that when he asks the Innkeeper if there's any room at the inn, and is told there isn't any room, I have visions of Joseph turning to Mary and confirming 'no, there isn't any room at the inn, babes!'

I was just wiping Little Angel Boy's face after his lunch (though a jet wash would be more appropriate) and I say to him 'it's movie night, tonight, son.'

His reply? 'I know, sweetheart.'

Alexis Carrington started crying earlier, saying her eye was sore. Daddy Shaun dutifully inspected her eye (and saw nothing untoward,) washed it out with saline, bathed it with a warm cloth and sympathetically advised her to rest it. He enquires a few minutes later 'is your eye feeling any better now, sweetheart?' She casually replies, without looking away from the TV, through a mouthful of Tesco's Finest mixed, cubed melon with 'yes, Dad, but it was my other eye that hurt, not the one you washed.'

Silly us.

December 9 2018

I just put on my Christmas jumper from last year, when I was slightly thinner. My jumper has got Rudolph's face on the front. After trying it on I realise Rudolph looks like he's had an allergic reaction to a peanut.

December 19, 2018

We've been asking the kids for months. 'What do you really want for Christmas?'

They have been unanimously answering 'I don't know,' for months.

We gave them Argos catalogues to circle what they would like - they gave us them back resembling fully completed colouring in books!

So, we had to narrow it down and choose for them. And believe me, they have a whole host of goodies to wake up to on the big day.

And now, with just 5 days to go, Alexis Carrington blurts out that she is expecting Santa to bring her a big talking green dinosaur. This is an area of interest she has NEVER mentioned or shown ANY interest in at ALL in her life. She decides that now is the time to drop this little bombshell on us.

Game. Changer.

December 23, 2018

Apparently, the best laugh you'll get out of your kids all year is to let out a massive pump and go 'oooh, I think a plop has come out!' Then shuffle towards the kitchen, pretending you've pooed yourself.

I am now a God in this house!

December 25, 2018

Woke up at 2am, 3am, 5am by an excited little fellow bouncing up and down on the bed going 'can we get up yet, can we get up yet????'

That was Daddy Shaun. The kids didn't wake up until half 6. I'm not even joking.

Merry Christmas, everyone.

January 1 2019

Up fresh as a daisy (not drinking is the way forward.) Feeling positive. Only one resolution this year - stop being fat! (Right after I finish another box of Lindor.)

I don't much care for new year, new me stuff. If you want to change something, you can do it whenever you like. It doesn't need a bookmark.

Just remember that if you've set any 2019 goal - enjoy the journey to it, rather than just focussing on the end result. Life is in the details. We're always in such a rush to get what we want or where we want to be that we forget to appreciate the ride. Take in the sights. Be grateful for the scenery.

Now... where's my Lindor stash?

January 4 2019

After the build-up and excitement of Christmas and New year, it's safe to say that Daddy Shaun is feeling a little gloomy so to cheer himself up, he decides, with a whole £80 in his bank account, that this is the year we are finally going to be wed. He books our wedding on the spur of the moment today and the date is set: Sunday 21st July 2019. He reassures me it will be a quiet affair. He said he can live without making his entrance by being dropped off in a helicopter, and he has promised to keep costs down. Which means he will tell me that things cost approximately half of what we have actually paid for them. He also reassures me that I will not have to do anything or lift a finger as he will take care of everything. The lying bastard.

Of course, this also means that I need to lose 5 stone in weight before we walk down that aisle. I can kill two birds with one stone to make a dent in the wedding fund and in my weight loss – does anyone want to buy one of my kidneys?

The kids are mega excited for the wedding when we announce it to them. That is until they realise that there isn't, in fact, going to be a bouncy castle and a soft play area for them to throw themselves around in all day. In fact, when we break that little nugget of information to them, Alexis tears up slightly, whilst, Little Angel Boy gives us a huffy 'AAAAWWWW.' However, Alexis perks right up as if we have wafted smelly salts under her scrunched-up nose when we inform her that she gets a brand new dress, shoes and some jewels as she will be our Flower Girl. She seems compensated and has paused her plans to write to her local MP about our wedding plans – for the time being! Little Angel Boy no longer cares either way as he has spotted a bird in the garden and he rushes out to terrorise it by screaming 'RAAAAAHHH' at it. The bird flies off, suitably scared, and Little Angel Boy comes in looking mighty proud of himself.

Daddy Shaun is making plans of his own to visit (terrorise) the local wedding decorator tomorrow. May God have mercy on her soul.

January 8 2019

Little Angel Boy came home from school and proudly announced he had been learning about The Soul Assistant at school. It took me a while to figure out he meant The Solar System. He's adamant he's correct and I'm stupid. Alexis Carrington informs me that our Sun is a star, and if we touch it - we will be dead. Yes, sweetheart. Yes, we will be.

January 11 2019

We always set the breakfast table the night before and Little Angel Boy arrived at the breakfast table this morning to see only Weetabix as the option for the day. There's usually two choices of cereal set out for them to choose from but both he and Alexis Carrington have only chosen Weetabix every day for about 6 weeks now. He enquires huffily 'DAD - there's nothing else - only Weetabix!!! I just need something else.' He trots along to the cereal cupboard to retrieve another breakfast option. I say to him 'but... you only ever have Weetabix, son.' He replies back 'I just need something else, Dad.'

He chooses Coco Pops and brings them to the table and sits down.

As I go to serve his breakfast, I say, just to be sure, 'So you're having Coco Pops, then?'

He puffs, quite calmly and innocently, his tone surprised at my apparent stupidity- 'No, Dad - I want Weetabix.'

My ears then started to bleed.

January 20 2019

'Alexa - 'eemind Daddy Shaun in 2 minutes he stinks of poo!'

Alexis Carrington is now dictating her memos for circulation through the digital realm.

January 25 2019

It was cheat night tonight and I had a kebab as my treat. I attacked it like a man possessed and now I'm sat in the chair so full and breathless and I feel like I should be saying 'there is no Dana only Zool' in a demonic voice

January 30 2019

I'm always a glutton for punishment, but eager for the punchlines, so I cautiously agree to the suggestion that we play I Spy around the dinner table tonight whilst having our tea. Little Angel Boy gets his turn and he says 'I spy with my little eye, something beginning with 'J''

We all have lots of guesses - juice, jumper, jam, jim-jams...'

He proudly replies 'nope!' to all our guesses. In the end we ask him for a clue.

He says 'OK... I'll give you a clue... it actually begins with 'H''

What a helpful clue.

February 21 2019

Alexis Carrington is bereft at misplacing one of her toys. This is her diary entry for today. She has reported it to the Police and a reward of a half-eaten packet of Haribos is on offer (belonging, (or rather belonged) to her brother, of course.)

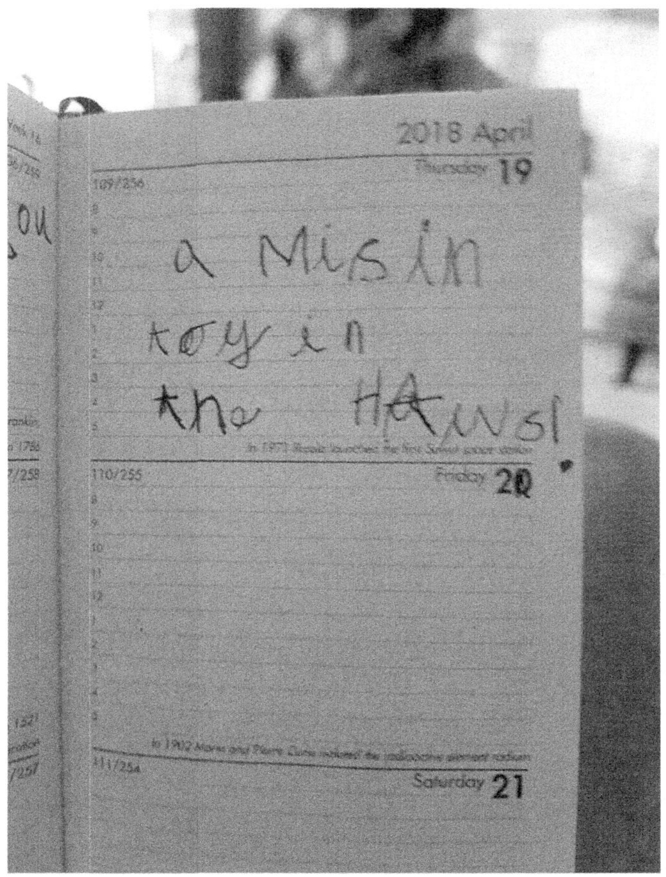

March 5 2019

Last night as I was drying Little Angel Boy after his little splash about in the bath, he started to loudly (and angrily) shout 'HEEEEEYYYYY.' Now, because he's been a temperamental and chewy little goblin for the past few days, I was expecting a full kick-off for no reason, because... well, for no other reason than he likes to keep us on our toes. So I sigh, and quickly mentally prepare myself for the spontaneous meltdown, but he follows his mega-horn 'HEEEEEEEYYYYY!!!' with an equally loud and impassioned 'SEXYYYYY BAY-BEEEEEYHH' He then breaks off into an interpretive dance which seems to channel a chicken having a fight with a duck; face scrunched up and eyebrows popping - giving his bare tush a right old shake across the landing. He was right into it.

It was the most hilarious thing.

Tonight, around the dinner table, he is being his usual loud little self, covered in barbeque sauce and using it as a face mask. Alexis Carrington, weary from at day of numbers and letters in the office, puts her hand on her head and pipes up with a withering 'John Paul! YOU are really, REALLY getting under my skin. Can you just shut up before I lose my appetite?!'

It was the most hilarious thing.

How funny are our kids?

March 10 2019

Movie night in the Davis-Webb household.

Alexis Carrington is tucking into her second snack pack of Butterkist, sat in between me and Daddy Shaun. Daddy Shaun lifts his leg to relieve himself of post-kebab gas. Alexis jumps up and declares 'I'm moving. You disgust me!' And off she trots to the cuddle chair in her Ugg slippers. Casting the occasional hacky look towards Smelly Dad.

March 24 2019

Alexis Carrington wanted to perform a song she's been working on. Her entrance on roller skates clutching her brand-new pink guitar set the mood for what would be an 'artistic' interpretation of Hall & Oates 'Maneater.' She followed it up with an equally interesting version of 'Tainted Love' by Soft Cell.

She'll be cutting a demo soon. Phoebe from Friends is shaking in her boots.

March 28 2019

School run. I live in a mad house, me

If anyone has any magazines or newspapers lying around, please could you have a scan through and keep any pictures of the Queen for me? Alexis Carrington has a school project for Easter, though I have a feeling she's just looking for tips on how to live like royalty. She's making a collage, or so she would have us believe. I have a sneaking suspicion that we should be expecting a new list of living demands in the coming days; complete with a presentation on how royalty, including Alexis, <u>should</u> be living.

April 30 2019

It's the kids school photo today. Daddy Shaun and Alexis Carrington misheard as they clearly headed to school today prepared for the Vogue Spring/Summer 2019 fashion photo shoot portfolio. Her hair has been teased and brushed and sprayed and she has taken more costume changes than a Cher concert to school with her. Morning wear and afternoon attire. The oversized sunglasses and lip gloss are ready, and she has had her nails done. Not one little bit spoiled.

Just in time for Little Angel/Goblin Boy's birthday, Daddy Shaun decides to surprise him (and Alexis) with…. A guinea pig each. YES! More pets. The kids are over the moon. Alexis Carrington decides to call her guinea pig Tilly Mae, whilst Little Goblin Boy thinks outside of the box by naming his new pet Batman. In the end, he settles for Batty Bullet as his guinea pig, which is black, turns out to be a girl and Little Goblin Boy loses all interest.

May 18 2019

Me: 'Someone left their Thor toy on the trampoline last night and it rained so he might not work now. This is why you need to look after your things.'

Little Goblin Boy (the artist formerly known as Little Angel Boy): 'I left Captain America out too, and he had his shield, so they'll be OK.' *blows raspberry*

Alexis Carrington chimes in: 'but you need to listen to dad and put things away.'

Little Goblin Boy: 'why don't you shut your mouth?'

Alexis Carrington: 'why do you keep telling me to shut up?'

Little Goblin Boy: 'I didn't. I told you to shut your stupid mouth.'

Me: 'don't speak to your sister like that!'

Little Goblin Boy: 'I love you, babes!'

We're in for a whole day of this

Daddy Shaun said he was unhappy about being rounder in the belly these days and Alexis Carrington pipes up with 'Dad you are carrot shaped. Not fat. Just focus on the carrot!'

Where does she get this stuff from?

Took my mother out shopping for her wedding outfit today. Now, I'm not saying our Barb is a talker, but we hadn't been in M&S more than 5 minutes and the poor old sales assistant my mam collared knew my mam's life history, the reason for our visit to the shops today, full exclusive details about my wedding- including who is invited and what she's having from the finger buffet on the evening - and she ended the conversation with 2 verses of her medical history and a chorus of what weight I was when I was born. By the time we left, the sales assistant looked 10 years older, my mam was out of breath and dehydrated and I was bad laughing.

Gotta love Barb.

Oh, and we walked the length of town and she didn't buy a thing. She's decided to look online. The online chat sales assistants are on red alert.

May 25 2019

Weekend justice:

Every day, to get up for school, we practically have to resuscitate Little Goblin Boy and coax him out of bed with a chocolate biscuit and empty promises at 8am.

However, on a weekend, Little Goblin Boy is doing somersaults backwards off the top of his wardrobe at 6am making all kinds of commotion.

Daddy Shaun, who loves a project, decides to completely re-jig Little Goblin Boy's bedroom and to create space he would like to re-mortgage the house to hire someone to harness the power of dark matter to create an interdimensional portal to gain this extra space in his bedroom. I suggested maybe a cabin bed.

May 26 2019

Little Goblin Boy's reign of terror continues.

He's been full of himself all day, and after the bath I sent him to put his PJ's on. I came downstairs and 10 minutes later there was still no sign of him, though I could hear what suspiciously sounded like a rhino stampede coming from his room. I shout up 'where are you? I've got your dessert ready!'

He was clearly put out by my enquiry and shouts back, huffily, 'ugh, I'm coming, you little peanut.'

I chuckled.

June 19 2019

We had a lovely big dinner tonight with a joint of pork and vegetables and it was all very civilised. The kids went off to play, while Daddy Shaun and I cleaned up afterwards.

After finally getting to sit down and have five minutes to ourselves, Alexis Carrington runs in from the garden. She announces that she is going to go for her after dinner poo. She inches her backside towards Daddy Shaun, and squeezes a little lady pump out in front of him and casually says 'I'll just leave that with you.' She then dashes upstairs to the toilet.

About 2 minutes later, Little Goblin Boy shouts down 'Daaaa-aaad! There's poo coming out of Lexi's bum!'

Knowing that the purpose of her little sprint upstairs, we just assumed that they were once again reminding us of the most hilarious subject in the world (to them) so we casually shout back 'OK!'

Again, Little Goblin Boy shouts downstairs 'Daaaa-aaaad. Lexi's got poo on the floor.' His tone suggests that he is quite amused, so we assume this is a little joke between the two of them upstairs. We ignore.

10 seconds later, a distressed panic call from Alexis bellows down stairs 'DAAAAAD!'

I dash up the stairs as fast as my chunky ankles can take my weight and walk into what can only be described as a 'scene' in the bathroom.

Little Goblin Boy is casually sat on the toilet, hands calmly clasped in front of him in his lap with a nonchalant little smile on his face. To the left of him, Alexis stands fully naked; her clothes strewn around the room as if she has ripped them off in a mad panic, and beside her, on the floor and up the bath is… a huge pile of turd.

Neither of them says a word. I look at Goblin. He looks at me smiling. I look at Alexis. She looks at me with a shocked face. I don't quite know what to say or exactly what I'm looking at. I stand there stunned and I stutter 'there's poo on the floor.'

No response.

'Oh my God, there's poo on the floor! Who did the poo on the floor?'

Little Goblin Boy proudly grasses his sister up (he's enjoying this too much) 'It was Lexi, Dad. She did a poo on the floor.'
Still not quite getting to grips with the sight before me, I ask, in a quietly stunned tone 'why? Why would anyone poo on the floor? Why would you poo on the bathroom floor???'

Alexis gets upset 'I'm sorry! I'm sorry!'

Again, bewildered I stand there and genuinely plead to know 'but…why would anyone poo on the floor???'

Alexis explains through tears that when she had announced her need to empty her bowels and dash up the stairs, Little Goblin Boy had decided that he would push her out of the way of the toilet and jump on before her to curl one out himself. This left Alexis, startled and with a turtle's head, and no other option but to take all her clothes off and have a poo on the lino because Little Goblin Boy wouldn't hurry up.

Indeed, I say to Little Goblin Boy – 'are you finished your poo?'

'Yep' he confidently replies.

'Hurry up and wipe your bum so Lexi can get on the toilet and I can clean her up,' I tell him.

Little Goblin Boy then moves slower than he ever has before and takes some toilet paper and painstakingly folds it into a perfect square and then moves his arm in slow motion towards his bottom. All the while relishing every moment of his sister's shame.

Meanwhile, Daddy Shaun has come upstairs to see what the fuss is about. He pops his head in, baulks then run's outside and I can hear him vomiting – loudly – into the hydrangeas.

I grab a carrier bag, don't ask me why, I figured I'd try and get this pile up and out into the bin. My hand slips on the floor and I get 'loose' stool all up my hand and arm. At this point my mouth starts to fill up with water. I dash downstairs to bin what was in the carrier bag, then back upstairs to scrub my arm with wire wool and bleach, to a distraught princess and giggling little goblin (who keeps taunting her 'why did you poo on the floor?')

Eventually we get everything cleaned up and we are all sat downstairs. Alexis has a glass of Evian water and a mint chocolate cornetto for her nerves. She's still a little upset by her ordeal. To make her feel better I tell her to go have a poo in the garden next time so we can all play hopscotch. She bursts out laughing. Her laughter turns to a scowl when I call her Princess Poo.

Me: 'I've made home-made burgers for tea. Who wants a slice of bacon with theirs?'

Alexis Carrington (holding back the tears): 'I just don't want the wet bits, Dad'

Me: 'OK, sausage, I'll cut the fat off for you.'

Little Angel Boy (hand up in the air - bursting with excitement and enthusiasm): 'Dad!!! I want the wet bits on my bacon and can I have hers too???'

My little caveman and Princess are such very different creatures.

July 7 2019

Daddy Shaun was instructing Little Goblin Boy to be on his best behaviour before we took him to a party this afternoon.

Daddy Shaun: 'John Paul can you listen to me, please? This is very important!'

Little Goblin Boy snaps back in his brattiest, cheekiest whine: 'I AAAAAMMMMM!'

Daddy Shaun: 'what did I just say, then?'

crickets

Daddy Shaun: 'see, so you weren't listening, were you?'

Little Goblin Boy: 'I was.'

Daddy Shaun: 'So what did I say?'

Little Goblin Boy: 'I know but I just don't want to say'

Obviously saving for our wedding has meant a few cutbacks in our house, so when Alexis Carrington asked for some dessert the other night, I fumbled around nervously in a blind panic trying to find something suitable and chocolatey. I discovered a Chunky Kit Kat (though thankfully not from my Emergency Stash) and I offered it to Alexis as I curtseyed and lowered my head as a knight would offer his sword to his queen in Game of Thrones - right before his head was swiftly removed. She scrunched up her little, freckled nose and made a baulking motion with her mouth as she waved her hands in front of her; ushering away the offending Chunky Kit Kat.

Well, I'm sorry, Princess, that we had no Ferrero Rocher or After Eights readily served on a China saucer with hand painted periwinkles, but times are hard. She instead plumped for fruit. Watermelon sliced into fans with the pips removed, if you please.

Brushing teeth before bedtime and I say to Little Goblin Boy 'I need to hear actual brushing, son, not just chewing your toothbrush.' He looks me dead in the eye and does not move his gaze as he literally moves the toothbrush less than a millimetre a minute across his mouth and I could see in his big brown eyes he thought he was getting one over on Daddy Trev. I didn't know whether to burst out laughing or flush my head down the toilet. The little wind up.

Little Goblin Boy had an announcement to make to Daddy Shaun and Daddy Trev this morning:

'Dad, I'm just going to tell you; I've got a girlfriend and I'm in love. We're going to get married. She's called Niamh.'

I like how he sat us down and broke the news to us like a Kay Burley exclusive for Sky News.

That evening, Alexis Carrington, clearly giddy with pre-wedding excitement, tells us that we should do something fun and just for Dads after the wedding as a treat. Her suggestion is soft play followed by the park. What a thoughtful idea, sweetheart. Yes - it's right on top of our list of things to do after our wedding. In fact, we were thinking about taking our Honeymoon at Lightwater Valley.

Our Wedding Day.

Almost 2 years to the day since we met our beautiful children, we booked our wedding day as close as possible to coincide with that particular anniversary.

The four of us arrived at our lovely little country venue just before 10am. Daddy Shaun was ushered off into one room with Princess Alexis Carrington to get dressed and I went to another room with my boy. I don't know how 1pm came so quickly but before I could blink, I had got us both bathed and dressed and it was time to get us down the aisle. I had said to him to be on his best behaviour today, as it was such an important day and he had to hold my hand when I did my speech as I was a bit nervous. I figured if I gave him this important job, it would stop him from being distracted. I met my gorgeous little girl at the bottom of the stairs in her beautiful green gown and sparkling tiara and I saw them both together, our only flower girl and page boy, looking so smart and proud to be by our side for our special day. They walked down the aisle first, Alexis and Little Angel Boy together, with Little Angel Boy carrying our rings. They looked so fantastic. I could hear the gasps of joy from our guests as they entered the room and walked the aisle. It was my turn next, with my Mam on my arm, I practically ran her down that aisle I was so nervous. The room was full of love for us all. It was practically tangible. I could feel the vibes and it sounds like a cliché, but it was absolutely electric. I stood at the front and watched as my husband to be walked down towards with his mam on his arm, with the biggest, brightest smile and tears in his eyes. He stood in front of me as we said our vows. It was just pure magic. Our little family unit was finally complete and today was the cherry on top. We would all have the same double-barrelled surnames after today. It felt like a natural bookend for this journey the 4 of us had taken. People often say it, but it really was one of the best days of our lives (it's right up there with the day we won Pizzas Hut Buffet vouchers with a free Ice Cream Factory. Just an FYI – I managed to lose 4 stone for our wedding day. Another FYI – what a fun weekend I had putting it all back on.)

When it did finally come to the speeches, and I stood up, very nervous, I felt a little hand wrap itself around my leg and I turned to see my son cuddling my leg as I spoke from the heart about my husband and children. He stood there on his chair next to me as I delivered the longest wedding speech ever recorded (25 minutes all told.) Watching the video back, I can see Alexis Carrington sat next to Daddy Shaun looking up at me as I spoke; she was transfixed and nodded in agreement with all the things I was saying, and interjecting with an occasional 'yep, yep!' as I continued. She looked so grown up. They both did. Our babies were so well behaved and so good all day long. It was a warm Summer's day and it was a long day, but they didn't complain once. In fact, Alexis wanted to give a little thank you to everyone herself over the microphone to our guests. It's fair to say, our children got the biggest applause of the day.

We had another little surprise up our sleeve for our first dance. For months, the four of us had been going to dance lessons every Friday evening to learn a family dance. Shaun and I wanted our first dance to be a family affair. That is who we are now. It's not just Shaun and I. It's all four of us. We're a team. The first dance was to the song 'Pure Imagination' which is a song from the Charlie and the Chocolate Factory movie. We chose it because if you listen closely to the lyrics, it tells a little bit of our story and our journey as a family. That particular journey, although it marks the end of this book, it actually signals a new chapter in our lives as we head off now feeling firmly united into the rest of our lives. Together. Forever.

If anyone out there is considering adopting children – DO IT. It will be the best decision you will ever make.

If you enjoyed this book, you will love the sequel by Trevor Davis-Webb – **'Two Dads, Two Kids'** is available to buy now, and is the next instalment in **'The Daddy Trev Diaries'** series.

Printed in Great Britain
by Amazon

27453357R00098